Not Another Meeting!

A Practical Guide for Facilitating Effective Meetings

Frances A. Micale

The Oasis Press®
Central Point, Oregon

To Jim
Without whom I still would have accomplished,
but not enjoyed the experience nearly as much!

Interior design by Eliot House Productions
Cover illustration and design by Steven Burns

Please direct any comments, questions, or suggestions regarding this book to

The Oasis Press®/PSI Research:
    Editorial Department
    P.O. Box 3727
    Central Point, Oregon 97502
    info@psi-research.com e-mail

The Oasis Press® is a Registered Trademark of Publishing Services, Inc., an Oregon corporation doing business as PSI Research.

Library of Congress Cataloging-in-Publication Data
Micale, Frances A., 1954 –
    Not another meeting : a practical guide for facilitating
effective meetings / Frances A. Micale – – 1st.ed.
    p. cm. – – (PSI successful business library)
Includes index.
ISBN: 1-55571-480-3 (pbk.)
1. Business meetings. 2. Meetings. I. Title. II. Series.
HF5734.5 .M53 1999
658.4'56 – – dc21   99–20270
                                               CIP

Printed and bound in the United States of America
First Edition 10 9 8 7 6 5 4 3 2 1
Printed on recycled paper when available

Table of Contents

Acknowledgments vi
Foreword by Peter A. Land vii

Introduction ix
    Managing the Meeting xiii
    Managing the Group xiv

Chapter 1   *How Do I Get Started?* 1
    Ensure a Meeting is Needed 2
    Preparing for the Meeting 3
    Beginning of the Meeting 8
    Body of the Meeting 11
    End of the Meeting 12
    Chapter Summary 15

Chapter 2   *I Thought I Knew How to Facilitate* 19
    What Is a Facilitator? 20
    Content Versus Process 22
    Content Neutral and Prccess-Oriented 23
    The Real World 27
    Chapter Summary 27

Chapter 3   *How Do I Get Them to Talk?* 29
    Exhibiting Active Listening 30
    Using Questions Effectively 33
    How to Ask Questions 34

Directing the Conversation Flow 36
The Flip Chart. 37
Signs of Good Communication 38
Chapter Summary 39

Chapter 4   *The Art of Facilitation* 43
Keeping the Group Aware. 44
When to Keep the Group Aware 45
Building Group Consensus 47
How to Build Consensus 50
What to Do When the Group Gets Stuck 51
When to Build Consensus 51
Maintaining Sensitivity and Flexibility. 53
Displaying Tactfulness 54
Chapter Summary 55

Chapter 5   *Let's Agree to Disagree*. 57
What Is Conflict 58
How Groups Respond to Conflict. 60
Interventions. 63
Types of Situations that Need an Intervention 65
Intervening to Gain Managerial Support 70
Chapter Summary 71

Chapter 6   *How Can We Get Things Done?* 73
Overview of PROBE. 74
How to Use PROBE 76
Develop a Projection 77
Examples of a Goal Statement. 78
Target the Root Cause of the Problem 80
List the Options 86
Choose the Best Option 91
Execute the Best Option 95
Chapter Summary 96

Chapter 7   *Should We Form a Team?* 99
Teams in Corporate America. 100
Enter the Facilitator 101
The Realities of Teams 101
How the Facilitator Helps 106
Team Development Stages. 108
Chapter Summary. 113

Chapter 8   *What Do I Do Now?* 117
             Case Situations 117
             Summary 140

Appendix A *The Case of Cable Express, Inc.* 127
             Cable Express, Inc. 127
             The First Meeting 128
             The Second Meeting 130
             The Fifth Meeting 136
             The Sixth Meeting 138
             Summary 140

Bibliography 143

Index 145

Acknowledgments

I sincerely thank the following people for taking the time to read and make suggestions.

Betty Bogusch	Cynthia Russell
Noel Burt	Deborah Peters
George Dahlberg	Beth Schumaker
Pete Land	Rich St. Dennis
Chuck Meeks	John Steed
Albert Micale	Sandy Stewart
Michael Micale	Heribert Stumpf
Bruce Nichols	Nicholas Tate
Robbie Roberson	Gary Wetherbee

A special thanks to Jerry Reynolds, my friend and mentor, who will always be with us in spirit.

I would also like to thank my publisher, Emmett Ramey, and my editor, Karen Billipp, for their help and support in producing a quality product.

Foreword

"Anything done well looks easy." I've heard this quote many times. How do we feel about star athletes, actors, or musicians who perform so magnificently with "effortless excellence?" I often feel admiration, adulation, and privilege to witness such outstanding contributions to ones' profession.

Those are the same feelings I experience when I watch Francie Micale conduct a meeting. When she is facilitating a session, the group quickly develops its own culture of professionalism, valued purpose, focus of ideas and a respectful exchange of facts, feelings and views. The most fascinating aspect of the event is that everyone knows that they are under the gentle but firm guidance of a consummate expert; it makes them rise to even higher levels of performance.

As I read this book, I could hear Francie speaking to a group of older men in the construction industry during a consulting engagement we conducted jointly a few years ago. Within minutes she had established rock-solid credibility with a group of "good old boys." Yes, the fact that she is very attractive and charming helped, but those assets were overshadowed by her superb skills in facilitating that two-day meeting.

The objective of this book is to share with you, the reader, the concepts, skills, and techniques that work so beautifully for her. As an international management consultant, I have seen very few facilitators in her class; she practices what she preaches.

All you have to do now is study, yes I said study, this book and apply what you will learn here when you facilitate your next meeting. If you do, you can expect it to be the best meeting you've ever attended and you will have fun doing it. Your group will say, "That meeting was conducted so well, it looked easy."

— Peter A. Land, President,
Peter A. Land Associates, Inc.

Introduction

*A*re you tired of attending endless meetings? Afraid of getting caught trying to sneak out? Concerned that someday you'll tell someone what you'd really like to do with his or her meeting agenda? Do you dread having to attend one more meeting in which you:

- Don't have a clue about why you're there?
- Waste a lot of time *not* making a decision?
- Get lost in the Bermuda Triangle of irrelevant discussions?
- Suffer through your boss' monologues?
- Gain ten pounds from eating too many donuts?
- Become exhausted because it's too long?

Unfortunately, complaints about the quality of meetings are very common. Since the time spent in meetings can be as much as 50 percent of the total work week, ineffective meetings can have a major impact on the success of an organization.

Why are so many meetings occurring in corporate America? In today's market, organization renewal and reinvention is critical in maintaining a competitive edge. The current level of change and upheaval has created the need to keep employees abreast of current events so they know and work toward the company's latest objectives. In addition, when addressing any business situation, ideas and opinions must be gathered in order to choose the best routes, and to maintain the level of personal commitment needed to reach challenging goals. Heribert Stumpf, Business Unit

Controller for Siemens in Atlanta, Georgia, says this about today's environment:

> Business today is more complex than ever. One person cannot always know what is the best decision. In many issues, getting others input through a team decision process is most effective in today's environment.

Gaining employee input whenever possible also increases the level of ownership, which in turn motivates employees toward making a stronger commitment to the business. This removes the handcuffs that limit people to only doing what is expected and unleashes the full potential in people so they can create a prosperous organization. One ideal arena for getting other's input and triggering a sense of ownership in people is the business meeting.

Since meetings can be so important to an organization, effectiveness and productivity become critical issues. Much of the responsibility for meeting success falls upon the person leading the session. It is therefore important to identify the possible functions of meetings.

Generally, meetings serve two major functions: sharing information or making decisions. Each function requires the person who is in charge of conducting the meeting to play a different role.

Sharing information requires the person conducting the meeting to take on a directive role, since the group is simply receiving information. This type of meeting represents the traditional meeting that has occurred in American companies for years and years. The person leading the meeting is there to present an idea or decision to the meeting attendees. He or she tells everyone else what to do and how it will be done. The meeting attendees are there to receive the information and carry out any directives given. For example, if there is a new policy, a meeting would be called to communicate the details to the appropriate people. Other types of information that would be presented would be the new structure of a re-organization, assignment of new jobs or responsibilities and announcement of a decision made by management. Staff meetings are common information sharing meetings because they are typically led by someone who presents current departmental events and performance. This type of meeting, while necessary at times, does not instill much commitment in people. People go to the meeting and carry out any directives given, but they are mostly doing what they are paid to do.

That's why the second meeting function, making decisions, has the potential to be much more powerful. Here meeting attendees are not just presented information, they are also asked to make a group decision about something that impacts the organization. This scenario creates more excitement in people because they know they'll have a voice in the process. They must utilize their expertise to explore possible options and choose the best options. They may also be given the authority to implement options selected.

When a group is in a meeting to make a decision, they are much more engaged in the meeting than when they are there to receive information. The group has been given the authority to participate, give ideas, and make and implement decisions. But, they need help in organizing their ideas and adding some structure around their efforts. A facilitator can fill this void.

The *facilitator* is the person designated to help the group make decisions, solve problems, and develop and implement plans within the structure of a meeting. The facilitator strives to create a comfortable atmosphere that encourages all members of the group to be actively involved during discussions. The facilitator can also help coordinate a group's efforts *outside* the meeting.

Several years ago, I learned the true significance of facilitation. I was hired to work with a medium sized company in the Atlanta area. I was asked to help the company become more customer focused and make some operational improvements. When I first started working with the management team, I noticed some common characteristics. They were not very excited about the prospect of working harder to make improvements in their work areas. Actually, they were downright unmotivated. Many were skeptical that they could get their people to make significant changes in how they did their jobs. I got the impression these managers did not like coming to work.

I knew I had a big job to accomplish, given the obstacles. I set to work scheduling and organizing problem-solving meetings. The idea was to facilitate the group and let them set the improvement schedule and actions needed to accomplishment their specified goals. During the meetings I tried to create an environment in which everyone had an opportunity to speak honestly and openly. All ideas were addressed in some way. At first there was a lot of silence, but when people started realizing they could speak their minds with no fear of reprisal, the group became fully engaged in the discussion. Little by little, the management team was able to work out their issues and problems. This extended into the front line employees, as well. Company communication improved, people became more proficient at solving problems, and morale improved.

There was one particular manager who changed dramatically. At first, he was the most skeptical and the most resistant toward the improvement effort. Yet, after attending the meetings, working closely with his peers, and seeing some of his own ideas being implemented, he realized that he could actually make a difference. He ended up being the biggest supporter of the improvement effort and was able to convince many other people to support the effort. They realized that they could really make a contribution and this resulted in many significant improvements in the company, including better customer service levels.

Effective facilitation is a key factor in helping people realize they *do* have a say and they *can* make a difference. The company I worked with described it quite well when they said that as a facilitator, I guided them through the change effort. The credit for actually making the improvements goes to the management team and all those involved in the improvement effort. They carried out the actions needed to make things better. I just pointed the way through the process.

The facilitator's role can be complex. Being an effective facilitator takes some practice and more effort. There is always something new to learn. This book will focus on how to facilitate groups to help them work together cohesively, and get results as they make business decisions.

Decisions can be made around two types of situations: business problems and business opportunities. A business problem is a situation in which something is not working properly. Examples are excessive errors in billing a customer, key entry errors, and service orders that are incorrect. Other examples include equipment breakdowns, excessive delays, poor customer service ratings, and low employee morale.

A business opportunity is a situation in which the group wants to enhance some aspect of the organization for future growth and development. There is no problem, but there is an existing opportunity that calls for a decision that will make the organization better or more competitive. For example, company managers may decide, based upon changes in the market or customer demands, that it is time to introduce a new product or service. Other examples would be if the decision is made to increase market share, plan an event, or develop a new ad campaign.

Business problems usually require a group to do some research on what is causing the problem. This activity, called root cause analysis, is necessary as a first step toward eliminating the problem. Business opportunities do not require root cause analysis because they do not deal with situations in which something has gone wrong.

An example of this difference would be if you had a dead tree in your yard. Before you go to purchase a replacement tree, you would do a root cause analysis to find out why the first tree died. If it was diseased, a new tree planted close by could also die. In this scenario, you are dealing with a problem. An example of an opportunity would be that you decide to purchase a new tree for your yard because you want to beautify your yard. Nothing has happened to any of your existing trees, you just want to add more foliage around your house.

In order to facilitate a group competently toward solving business problems or addressing business opportunities, there are two things you must be able to manage: the meeting and the group in attendance.

Managing the Meeting

In order to manage a meeting effectively, you need to do three things. First, you must ensure that a meeting is even needed. It is amazing how many times I hear complaints about the number of unnecessary meetings that are scheduled in organizations. Nick Tate, editor for science and medicine at the *Atlanta Journal and Constitution* says, "Often someone will say we need to schedule a meeting to discuss a specific issue. I always make a point of asking if it would be possible to discuss the issue right now, while we're together. Many times, I am able to avoid having to schedule a meeting. That saves both parties a lot of time." This book will give you some additional tips and alternatives to make sure you don't schedule unnecessary meetings.

The second action that must be taken is to prepare adequately for the meeting. It is great to have the visibility you get from being in charge of running a meeting. However, it is *not* so great to get the visibility when you are not prepared and everyone in attendance notices. This can reduce the amount of importance being placed upon the issues being discussed and place you in an unfavorable light. You will learn the specific steps necessary for preparing thoroughly without spending an inordinate amount of time.

The third necessary action is conducting the meeting. The ensuing chapters will focus on several aspects of this. You will learn the specific steps for both beginning and ending a meeting. You will also learn ways to structure a group's approach toward reaching a specified goal.

Managing the Group

The second area is effectively managing the group. There are four competencies that will help you do this. The first competency is remaining content neutral. This means being completely unbiased about the ideas and opinions the group is expressing. This is sometimes difficult to do: it requires self-discipline. As a consultant, the groups I facilitate are quick to let me know when I am not being neutral. They don't need my opinions, only my guidance in leading them through the meeting agenda. It sometimes takes considerable effort to remain silent, but the group's *positive* response is much preferred over a *negative* response (such as telling me to butt out, or rolling their eyes).

Being a content neutral facilitator is similar to being a conductor for an orchestra. The legendary Arturo Toscanini conducted symphonies all over the world. He directed the flow of music, just as a facilitator directs the flow of conversation. However, Mr. Toscanini never played an instrument as he conducted, just as a facilitator never states his or her own opinion while facilitating.

The second competency is facilitating the discussion. There is nothing worse than asking a question and getting silent stares from the group. The opposite response could also occur. This is known as sheer pandemonium. You ask a question and everyone talks at once. Betty Bogusch, Ph.D., an instructional design consultant, must be able to conduct an effective discussion in a variety of group situations, whether the group is quiet, vocal, or a combination of both. "I do whatever it takes to get my groups involved. I help them find commonality among themselves with the use of icebreakers. This usually makes them more comfortable stating their views. I also make a point of talking to quiet people during breaks and asking specific people to present relevant topics at the next session, or the next day. It's important to open up the discussion to everyone, not just the one or two vocal individuals." You will learn techniques for making it easy for group members to participate and keep an orderly discussion. When this is done effectively, people will realize they can make a contribution and will be more encouraged to participate.

The third competency is applying the bird's eye view, which means observing what is happening with the group and determining how well the group is working together. A good facilitator also constantly assesses his or her own level of effectiveness. Is the group on schedule and focused on the current agenda item? The group needs an objective person to point out what is happening. You will learn specific ways to identify what is happening and what to say to make the group aware of what is happening.

The last competency is managing conflict. The focus is on managing conflict, not eliminating conflict. The facilitator is there to help people express their views openly and honestly. This can help increase the group's commitment to a particular decision because it gives people a chance to discuss their views, even if some group members do not agree. You will learn to encourage disagreement so the group can address all concerns and effectively make a decision that all group members can support.

This book will begin with the more basic concepts first. Chapter 1 will concentrate on the actions necessary to manage the meeting. It will describe how to prepare for a meeting, including how to set the goal for a meeting and the proper way to develop an agenda. Chapter 1 also describes the five steps for opening a meeting and the steps required to summarize and close a meeting.

Chapters 2 through 5 will concentrate on important skills for managing the group.

Chapter 2 will focus on the importance of neutrality and will give you specific examples to clarify what it means to be neutral. Chapter 3 will teach you how to effectively facilitate the discussion to get equal involvement from all group members. Chapter 4 will discuss how to identify how well the group is working together and ways to communicate your observations. Chapter 5 will explain how to effectively manage conflict and help the group reach agreement even when they have reached an impasse.

Chapter 6 will focus on the two types of decisions groups work on — business problems and business opportunities. You will learn a method that will help structure a group's approach toward either solving a problem or addressing an opportunity. You will also learn about root cause analysis in this chapter.

Chapter 7 will discuss the dynamics of formal teams: how they work together, what they can accomplish, and how the facilitator can help. You will get some helpful tools such as the Team Planning Form for starting a brand new team and the Team Mission/Objectives Form to help identify the business reasons for a team's existence.

xvi / *Not Another Meeting!*

Chapter 8 and Appendix A will help you apply the concepts in this book. Chapter 8 will give you a series of difficult situations in which you will identify appropriate facilitator responses, then check your answer against the book's answer. Appendix A takes you through a case situation, where you will see the concepts in this book applied to a fictitious organization.

All you have to do is study each chapter and apply the information. You will learn the principles taught in this book by taking the time to understand what is being discussed and doing the exercises at the end. You will find reinforcement for those skills you are already practicing. Ultimately, your organization will win and so will you personally.

You can break the pattern of ineffective meetings in your organization. You'll stop hearing people say, "Not another meeting!" and you'll start hearing, "This is too important to skip!" You will be contributing significantly to your organization, and ultimately, to syour own career.

1

How Do I
Get Started?

Gina, a call center manager, sits at her desk, wondering how she got herself into the mess she is in. She is being given *more* things to do. She is now in charge of the staff meetings, and she's got one coming up this week. Everyone hates staff meetings, and now Gina is under the gun to "make them more productive," as her boss puts it.

The group is really going to groan when she tells them about this meeting coming up. It's a busy time of year. But, there have been an excess of billing errors occurring in the last three months. They are 20 percent higher than normal. Customer Service Reps (CSR's) have been receiving more customer complaints as well. Gina knows when she presents this information to the group, they will realize the importance of the meeting and respond accordingly. After all, they are the call center managers. Each manager supervises 20 CSR's. An opportunity to reduce billing errors would certainly make all of their jobs easier.

Gina's boss, John Hegate, has asked the group to identify possible causes of the billing error problem. Since the group is so busy with their regular responsibilities, he will take the next steps after they identify these possible causes.

*A*lthough she is pressed for time, Gina is confident she can organize and conduct the meeting because she knows the appropriate process to follow.

There are some simple practices that, if followed, can significantly improve a meeting.

This chapter will show you how Gina conducts a well-organized meeting by preparing the meeting objective and developing an agenda. You will also get tips on how to make your meetings more productive by effectively beginning a meeting, closing a meeting, and keeping the group closely aligned with the meeting agenda.

Ensure a Meeting Is Needed

Before this meeting is scheduled, Gina has to make sure a meeting is warranted to fulfill the objective. The last time Gina was asked to hold a meeting, she decided against doing so. It was when John wanted the group to decide on a new copy machine. Gina had already discussed each person's preferences and the group was generally in agreement. Gina sent out an e-mail to each group member to confirm their individual choices, which eliminated the need for holding a meeting.

This upcoming meeting is being scheduled to identify potential causes of billing errors. So, Gina considers alternatives to holding a meeting. She could get their ideas using e-mail, a memo and even a phone call. The disadvantage to these alternatives is that group members would not be able to discuss these billing errors with each other in person. A live discussion might generate understanding about the problem and some additional potential causes of the problem.

Another alternative might be a brief one-on-one discussion between Gina and each group member. That might prove very time consuming. Also, this alternative is more suited to a situation when the subject is confidential or sensitive. The issue of billing errors needs to be discussed openly and honestly. There is the potential for people to feel they are being blamed, so the group as a whole should take ownership of the problem.

One other possible alternative to holding a meeting is having a brief stand-up discussion. Gina reasons that this would be effective when the meeting objective can realistically be achieved in 15 minutes or less. Discussing billing error causes will take longer, probably 45 minutes. Standing up for that length of time would be distracting and annoying for the group members.

Gina realizes that meetings can be expensive, considering the average cost. So, she calculates the meeting cost by multiplying the group's average hourly wage times the number of meeting attendee's times the estimated amount of time the meeting will last. The example below shows her calculations.

$30.00 (average hourly wage) x 8 group members = $240

$240 x .75 (¾ of an hour stated as a percentage) = $180 (cost of meeting)

If people are in a meeting, then they cannot perform work-related duties. Thus, the group's loss of productivity is also considered. There may be other costs involved, such as renting a room to meet in and any refreshments and supplies needed.

In addition, Gina weighs the meeting cost against its possible benefits: a first step in eliminating errors that customers receive when they are billed for service. Gina realizes that billing errors have the potential to alienate customers, drive some customers away and decrease productivity when a CSR has to spend time correcting an error because it was not done right the first time. All of these issues tie in closely with the company's business objectives. This meeting is obviously well worth the investment.

Preparing for the Meeting

Gina knows that many meetings either succeed or fail before they ever take place, based upon what happens during the preparation phase. Her preparation will take approximately 30 minutes. First, she will need to identify the objective for the meeting and create a statement that clearly describes what the group will accomplish by the end of the meeting. This is called the meeting outcome statement. Next, Gina will develop a sequence of steps the group will take to reach the outcome. This is the meeting agenda. Lastly, Gina will consider who needs to be invited.

A meeting without an objective is like taking a trip into the twilight zone. If you've ever attended a meeting in which there was no stated agenda, you understand what is meant by the "twilight zone." There's no purpose, therefore there is no way to focus on any one subject. People end up leaving the meeting wondering what was accomplished.

That's why it's so important to identify the intended outcome as your first step toward preparing for the meeting. A *meeting outcome statement* is a statement of purpose that describes what the group must achieve. It identifies a concrete, specific, and tangible outcome; such as arriving at a decision, developing a solution, creating a list, or designing a plan. The meeting outcome statement should be presented every time there is a meeting, to clarify the purpose of the gathering. It should be written before the meeting begins, posted during the meeting, and constantly referred to throughout the session.

A meeting outcome statement should be clear and it should hold the group accountable for reaching an objective. To accomplish this, always write the outcome statement in a way that indicates the desired result has already been achieved. This is done by first identifying the actual result that will be reached by the end of the meeting. Place this at the front of the statement. Figure 1.1 contains a list of common results that are achieved in meetings. It is possible to have more than one anticipated result. However, avoid doing too much in a limited amount of time. It may be better to schedule two meetings instead of trying to squeeze too much into one meeting.

After the actual result is identified, a brief description to clarify the result should follow. For example, imagine the group is asked to choose 20 books to purchase and place in the company library. First, examine Figure 1.1 and

---

Figure 1.1

Results Used in
Meeting Outcome Statements

A List

A Solution

A Decision

A Plan

A Flow chart

A Proposal

A Goal Statement

A Survey

---

choose the result that most closely describes the group's anticipated goals. They must build a list of book titles, so the outcome statement should begin with, "A list". Then, a description of the type of list should follow. The following outcome statement accurately reflects what they need to accomplish during the meeting.

A list of 20 book titles for the company library.

This statement makes it clear that the group will decide which books to put in the library. It is also easy to tell whether the intended outcome was accomplished by the end of the meeting. The group will either have a list of 20 books, or not.

Here is another example: A group is trying to choose between two equipment vendors that have submitted proposals. Everyone has read the proposals and met with the vendors. The group must reach an agreement on which vendor will be maintaining and repairing equipment. First, choose the result in Figure 1.1 that best describes what needs to be accomplished during the meeting. In this case, the word "decision" is the most accurate description of what will occur. Then, provide a description of the type of decision that will occur. Here is the best meeting outcome statement for this situation.

A decision on an equipment vendor for maintenance and repair.

Another example involves plant employees who must develop a schedule to keep the plant running, either during outages caused by bad weather or other unexpected circumstances. The most descriptive result in this situation is a plan. Here is the outcome statement.

A plan for maintaining plant operations during outages.

When the above meeting is held, everyone will clearly understand what they are to accomplish and how much they will need to get done within the time frame of the meeting.

Concerning Gina's situation, she considers her upcoming meeting and its goals. The group is asked to identify what is causing the billing errors that customers have been complaining about. The most appropriate result is a list. Gina adds a descriptive phrase that explains the type of list to be developed.

A list of possible causes of billing errors experienced by customers.

This intended outcome accurately reflects what the group will accomplish by the end of the meeting. It also makes it easier for Gina to take the next step, which is writing the agenda for the meeting.

Some people wonder why an intended outcome and an agenda is so important to a meeting's success. The *meeting agenda* is the "road map" used by the facilitator to chart the steps the group will follow to achieve the intended outcome for the session. Once the desired outcome is identified, an agenda is needed to show the group what needs to be done to achieve the meeting outcome.

This is the same concept as using a map to find a destination. My husband Jim and I love to take excursions on our boat in beautiful Perdido Bay in Orange Beach, Alabama. Jim drives the boat and I help him navigate. If we have a certain destination (or intended outcome) in mind, we follow a map (or agenda) very closely so we will reach it within an acceptable amount of time.

This example explains why many groups have trouble making progress in meetings. Often an intended outcome or destination is not identified. So, the group gets off track easily or becomes confused. They take the scenic route, as Jim and I do when we don't have a particular destination in mind. If an agenda is not used during a meeting, this is also a detriment because the group will not have anything to guide them toward their intended outcome. Both an outcome and an agenda are needed to get the group to its destination. The outcome is developed first, to pinpoint the destination. Then the agenda is developed to chart the steps needed to reach the destination.

The agenda should be posted and referred to during the meeting. It can also be sent out ahead of time. You may choose to develop a detailed agenda for your own personal use (such as the one in Figure 1.2), and create a less detailed agenda for the participants.

When you develop a detailed agenda, begin with writing down the intended outcome, the time scheduled for the meeting, the place and who will be present. This is shown in the top section of Figure 1.2. Also shown here is the list of meeting attendees. Limit the number of meeting attendees to those who contribute information, or those who are impacted by what is discussed in the meeting. If appropriate, also invite those who can provide support. If a key person can only be present for part of the meeting, organize the agenda topics around the time that person is present.

Figure 1.2

Meeting Agenda

Expected Outcome: A list of possible causes of billing errors experienced by customers

Date: March 3

Time: 2:00 P.M.

Place: Conference room, 2nd floor

Who Should Attend: J. Loom, J. Caravell, F. Black, C. Douglas, B. Williams, L. Gunther, J. Hegate, A. Toll, L. Tomas, J. Towey,

What	Time	Who
Beginning of the Meeting		
Welcome the group	30 seconds	
Clarify the outcome	3 minutes	John Hegate
Set role expectations	1 minute	
Establish ground rules	30 seconds	
Discuss agenda	30 seconds	
Body of the Meeting		
Brainstorm possible causes	18 minutes	
Clarify causes	10 minutes	
Eliminate unnecessary causes	10 minutes	
End of the Meeting		
Summarize against outcome	30 seconds	
Verify action items	30 seconds	
Praise the group's effort	30 seconds	

The meeting agenda is divided into three columns — What, Time, and Who. *What* refers to the proposed topic, or what the group will be doing. *Time* is the estimate of how much time is needed to cover each agenda item. The *Who* column is used to note the names of guest speakers, or to indicate that someone other than the facilitator will make a presentation to the group. The agenda in Figure 1.2 indicates that John Hegate will be a guest speaker. He is only there to answer any questions about the problem. He is the one who initiated this improvement effort, so he wants to make sure the group understands what is expected. After questions are answered, he will leave so that they can work without any interference from him.

Concentrate on the "What" column first because this is where you identify topics or actions needed to progress toward the intended outcome. There are five steps listed under the "What" column in Figure 1.2. They describe the steps a facilitator takes to begin a meeting. You should always begin your meetings with these five steps.

Beginning of the Meeting

There have been numerous occasions when group members have approached me at a break and said, "I am getting a lot out of this meeting. That doesn't surprise me because you started out very effectively." Beginning a meeting effectively and thoroughly is not difficult, you just have to guide the group through five steps. These steps may be covered in depth, or very quickly, depending upon how formal the meeting is and how often the group has met together in the past. If the group "knows the routine," follow them quickly without compromising a clear understanding of future topics.

At the beginning of the meeting, you should create a positive tone by:

- Welcoming the group.
- Conducting any necessary introductions if participants don't know each other.
- Making sure the group knows the location of restrooms and phones, announcing when the meeting will end and covering other logistical issues.
- Referring to any action items that should have taken place at a previous meeting.

A proper welcome sets a positive tone for the rest of the meeting. Participants who sense that you are organized and in control will place more importance on the time that is being spent for the meeting. Of course this also includes starting the meeting on time, and ending it on time. By beginning a meeting at the published time, you go very far in establishing credibility with the group. Ending the meeting on time ensures that everyone present is willing to give their full attention to the meeting topics as opposed to wondering when the meeting will end! Time is precious to all. Respect it.

Next, you should clarify the intended outcome for the meeting by:

- Posting the outcome for the group.
- Describing any parameters surrounding the outcome, as well as any useful background information. *Parameters* are limits that the group must work within, including deadlines, budget constraints or consequences of the project at hand.
- Ensuring that the group understands the intended outcome by asking for questions.
- Referring to the intended outcome as the meeting progresses so that the group remains focused.
- If the meeting is part of an ongoing project, summarize which step the group is currently focusing on.

Once the meeting outcome is clarified, the group should have no question about why they are present or what should be accomplished. It is easier to keep the group on track by reminding members of the intended outcome.

Setting role expectations is the next step for beginning a meeting. This is done so that everyone knows what they should do to make the meeting a successful one. Start out with your role.

My name is _____ and I'm going to be your facilitator today. I will help you work more effectively toward your intended outcome by helping you create a list of the causes of billing errors. I will make suggestions to help you get there faster, but I won't contribute my opinion on what you should do to reach the outcome. If you find that I am too involved and am getting in the way, please let me know.

Of course, in most instances, the group will already know you, so there won't be a need to be quite as formal as the example here. It is most important the group comprehends your role when you are facilitating, since this role can be misunderstood.

There are other roles that you might want to fill during the meeting, depending upon the meeting outcome. One way to fill any of these roles is to ask for volunteers. You are still responsible for managing people who take on these roles so that they are helpful and don't become a hindrance. These roles are listed here:

> **Recorder:** Normally, the facilitator records ideas on an easel. If the group is very large (more than fifteen participants), or if the facilitator chooses, one person can serve as recorder and concentrate on *boarding* ideas so the facilitator can focus on conducting the discussion. Boarding ideas means writing down the groups ideas on a flip chart for everyone to view it.

> **Timekeeper:** The timekeeper keeps track of time as the meeting progresses. This is important because it prevents the group from spending too much time on an issue and ending the meeting without reaching the outcome. A good timekeeper periodically points out the group's progress and compares it to the estimated time frames for each agenda item.

> **Co-facilitator:** When the number of meeting participants is greater than 15, two people can take turns facilitating. While one facilitator is conducting the meeting, the other keeps the group focused by quietly breaking up sidebar conversations.

> **Coordinator:** The coordinator handles meeting logistics, such as booking the meeting room, sending out memos announcing the time and place, and handling the refreshments for breaks and lunch.

> **Minutes Taker:** The traditional duty of the minutes taker is to write down a summary of decisions made. This could include writing down the flip chart notes that are boarded by the facilitator. If the group is discussing a lot of detailed information that must be passed on to people outside the meeting, asking for someone to take detailed discussion notes might also be helpful.

Participants also have a meeting role; they should be encouraged by you to ask questions, participate, and follow the ground rules.

Ground rules are established to help meeting participants work together more effectively. You may present ground rules that you develop ahead of time, or, time permitting, ask the group to develop its own, and if the same group is meeting on a regular basis. Develop ground rules that specify behaviors to help make the meeting more successful, such as:

- be on time;
- avoid interrupting others;
- participate;
- respect others' opinions; and
- do not engage in personal attacks.

After presenting the ground rules, secure the group's commitment to following them. This is called *contracting* with the group:

> "These are our ground rules. Do I have everyone's commitment that you will follow these guidelines?"

Once members agree to following the ground rules, it is easier to enforce the rules should the need arise. If members do not agree with the ground rules, ask them to make whatever changes are necessary so they *can* commit to them.

The last step for beginning a meeting is to present the agenda. Briefly discuss the agenda and ask if there are any questions or points that need clarification. This will show the participants what has to happen in order to reach the outcome. The agenda should also be posted or handed out and referred to throughout the meeting.

Body of the Meeting

After you cover the agenda, you have completed the five steps for beginning the meeting. That was just the appetizer. It sets the stage for the entree or real work of the meeting, also referred to as the body of the meeting. This work becomes the middle of your agenda, shown in Figure 1.2. The steps for beginning a meeting are typically the same for all meetings. Steps covered in the body of a meeting agenda are different from one meeting to the next, because the intended outcome is usually not the same.

Develop the middle of your agenda with your meeting outcome statement in mind. What does the group have to do to reach the intended outcome? Your agenda should consist of the steps needed to accomplish the desired outcome. For example, Gina's intended outcome is a list of possible causes of billing errors. She reasons that the group will most likely brainstorm all the causes they have observed and learned about through the CSR's comments and customer complaints. Gina also knows John Hegate will use the list to see which causes occur most often. The list might need clarification, so that John understands each cause completely.

Gina decides to begin with asking the group to *brainstorm* a list of billing error causes. Brainstorming occurs when people give ideas on a particular subject without deciding if the idea is a good one or a bad one. The list may end up with some causes the group decides to remove later. However, brainstorming will ensure that none of the important causes are left out.

As shown in Figure 1.2, the next step after brainstorming is to *clarify* the list of causes. Clarifying means explaining the meaning of an item on the list. Gina will ensure that any items not understood by a group member are explained by its originator.

The next step is to eliminate any unnecessary causes on the list. This is possible only after the group understands the items through clarification. Gina asks them if any causes can be deleted from the list once it is sent to John Hegate.

Once the group has agreed that the list accurately reflects current billing error causes, they have met their outcome. Gina is now ready to end the meeting.

End of the Meeting

The way a meeting ends sets the tone for fulfilling the planned decisions. If the group did not achieve the goal specified in its outcome statement, group members can decide to extend the meeting or schedule another one. This is a group decision, since it is your responsibility to end the meeting on time. Only the group members can take responsibility for extending the planned ending time.

When the group is satisfied the intended outcome was accomplished, you are ready for the first step needed to end a meeting, called summarizing. Discuss what was accomplished or decided during the session and revisit any unfinished business.

- Reiterate any decisions made, or any progress toward the outcome.
- Discuss any issues that were not yet resolved; ask the group members how they want these issues handled.
- Set the date, time, and place of the next meeting.

To verify action items at the end of a meeting, you must be prepared during the entire course of a meeting. As a typical meeting progresses, members often point out actions needed during the course of the discussion. Make a point of noting all commitments made by group members, as well as any action items that were established. Then, as the meeting wraps up, verify who will do what and by what date the task will be completed. These action items also should be revisited at the next meeting if appropriate.

Another important step for ending a meeting is to praise or thank the group for a job well done. This will help end the meeting on a positive note. Of course, handle it with sincerity. Try to identify specific ways the group worked together effectively, accomplished their intended outcome within the time limits, listened well, or persisted through a challenging process.

What you do after the meeting to follow up is as important as what you do during the meeting. You may need to check with group members who volunteer to accomplish agreed-upon tasks. If there was a request for additional information during the meeting, you may be the person responsible for getting the information and communicating back to the group. You also need to notify appropriate people of any decisions made during the meeting.

Publishing meeting results is an important part of follow-up. Shortly after the meeting, write up a brief summary of the meeting highlights. Point out what progress was made toward the designated outcome. Include the action items that were set, including who is responsible for each action, and by what date the action should be completed. If there are any misunderstandings, individual participants can then contact you in order to clarify their role or their understanding of the meeting outcome.

Another important follow-up activity is to evaluate the meeting's effectiveness. Obtaining feedback about your skill in facilitating the meeting is important. First, complete a self-evaluation on your own handling of this meeting. Figure 1.3 can be used for this purpose. Review this checklist of the steps for facilitating a meeting effectively. Evaluate your own role in

Figure 1.3

Meeting Facilitation
Self-Evaluation Form

Ensuring a Meeting is Needed

❏ Did I determine the purpose for the meeting?

❏ Did I compare alternative methods for fulfilling the purpose?

❏ Did I evaluate the cost for the meeting?

❏ Did I consider business objectives in deciding whether or not to call a meeting?

Preparing for the Meeting

❏ Did I write a meeting outcome statement?

❏ Did I invite the right people?

❏ Did I decide the meeting time?

❏ Did I choose the location (and reserve the space, if necessary)?

❏ Did I write the meeting agenda?

❏ Did I create and distribute the agenda?

Beginning of the Meeting

❏ Did I welcome the participants?

❏ Did I clarify the meeting outcome?

❏ Did I discuss any roles needed?

❏ Did I establish ground rules?

❏ Did I discuss the agenda?

Body of the Meeting

❏ Did I lead the group through the planned agenda?

Did I successfully handle the discussion by:

❏ using active listening?

❏ using questions effectively?

❑ directing the conversation flow so all participated?

❑ displaying tactfulness?

❑ letting the group make the decisions?

❑ Did I keep the meeting on track?

End of the Meeting

❑ Did I summarize progress toward the meeting outcome?

❑ Did I verify action items?

❑ Did I congratulate group members on efforts and accomplishments?

Follow Up

❑ Did I follow up on action items?

❑ Did I obtain feedback on meeting facilitation skills?

❑ Did I use the feedback to improve my meeting facilitation skills?

---

successfully completing each of the steps. Think through the facilitation skills. Which ones did you handle particularly well? Congratulate yourself on your efforts. Then choose one skill area where you think you could improve. Decide what you need to do to improve this skill the next time.

Obtain feedback from the other participants. Either ask them personally what you did well and how you need to improve, or request they give you written feedback either in a memo or through e-mail.

Use the feedback to continuously improve your facilitation skills. You'll be amazed at the improvement in productivity and reduced participant frustration, as a result of your new meeting facilitation skills.

Chapter Summary

Your Prescription for Better Meetings

The techniques in this chapter are fundamental in ensuring that your meetings are structured to *get something done!* The following chapter summary presents the basics for meeting effectiveness.

Ensure a Meeting is Needed

Always make sure a meeting is the appropriate response to what you are trying to achieve. There are other alternatives, such as using e-mail, making phone calls, conducting one-on-one discussions or having brief stand-up meetings. Calculating the actual cost of a meeting and comparing the intended outcome against company business objectives can also clarify whether a meeting is the best alternative.

Prepare for the Meeting

The effectiveness of a meeting is impacted by how much the facilitator prepares in advance. It's important to ask yourself the following questions:

- Is there a meeting outcome statement?
- Is there an agenda?
- Are the right people invited?

Beginning of the Meeting

The following steps for beginning a meeting should always occur, both formally and in detail, or informally and briefly:

- Welcome the group, make necessary introductions and check the status of previous action items.
- Clarify the meeting outcome.
- Set role expectations.
- Contract the ground rules.
- Present and describe the meeting agenda items, so the group knows what is happening during the session.

Applying these steps ensures that the group members have a good understanding of why the meeting is taking place, what is expected of them, and how they will reach the intended outcome.

Body of the Meeting

The body of the meeting is where the actual work toward the intended outcome takes place. Ideally, progress toward the desired result of the meeting moves in a logical, efficient manner. What the group actually works on depends on the specific intended outcome.

End of the Meeting

A good summary at the end of a session caps off what has been accomplished and verifies what the group agreed to during the meeting. You should:

- Point out progress against the outcome.
- Verify any action items.
- Praise the group's effort.

After the meeting is over, remember to:

- Follow up as necessary.
- Publish the results of the meeting.
- Evaluate the meeting's effectiveness.

Practicing these fundamentals ensures that your meetings are on track and productive. As Gina learned, the reputation of being an effective meeting facilitator ensures that you will get impressive levels of attendance, full participation, and solid support of decisions made in all your meetings!

2

I Thought I Knew How to Facilitate

Rob is a plant manager who has been assigned the facilitator's role for his departmental quarterly meeting. Rob is excited about the prospect of leading the group in the right direction. He's been with the company for 21 years and feels that he can really make a positive contribution. The group was asked to make several decisions, but he's sure he can steer them in the right direction. He has more experience than most of the group members and they look up to him. He expects that the group will accomplish a lot if he can get them to do what he knows is best for the company.

Rob will definitely make an impact — probably the wrong one. It is clear that he intends to lead and expects the group to follow. Yet, since the whole group is charged with making the decisions, and Rob was assigned the role of facilitator, he should avoid stating his own opinions. Otherwise, group members may end up wondering why they're involved if one person is making all the decisions!

There are some common misconceptions about facilitation. Well-meaning individuals, like Rob, often take on the role of facilitator without really understanding what this role involves. The true facilitator should be neutral on all issues and avoid giving personal opinions. Also, meeting participants sometimes mistakenly believe that the facilitator should tell the group what to do. If the group has been given the authority to make a decision or share input, then the person leading the meeting must facilitate and maintain neutrality.

This chapter will explore the issues around facilitator neutrality. You will learn when it's appropriate to give your opinion and when it's not. There are several examples that will be discussed so that you will understand how to communicate clearly while focusing on how the group is working together. This information will help you facilitate with neutrality and encourage your groups to take responsibility for solving problems and addressing opportunities.

What Is a Facilitator?

A *facilitator* is someone who helps groups work together to make decisions, develop plans, and then implement those plans. This description implies that it is the group that is responsible for the decision making, planning and implementation. The facilitator simply *makes it easy* for the group to carry out its function. This distinction between the facilitator and the group is an important one, because it clarifies the roles and responsibilities for all involved. While the facilitator is responsible for making it easy for the group to perform, the group is responsible for its own success. The group must ultimately answer to management: What was accomplished?

Choosing a facilitator requires careful consideration. The facilitator could be anyone: the group leader, the manager, or a group member. However, the best person for the job is usually the one who can easily take a neutral part in the group's work. It is easier to facilitate if you do not have any strong opinions about the specific project the group is working on, or if you are able to keep quiet about personal opinions.

Here is another example:

> Judy manages a group of 12 people in network operations. The group writes methods and procedures for the rest of the company. Members are currently revamping one of the methods that was put into practice five years ago. They were told that their collective recommendation would be implemented. Judy has some specific ideas about how this method should be revised, so she decides to facilitate the process, so she can give her input.

In this example, Judy is clearly not the best person to facilitate because she has specific ideas about what she wants the group to accomplish. There are two obvious problems. First, Judy will probably end up controlling the group's decisions, even though members expect to have the authority to make decisions themselves. The facilitator's role carries a certain amount of authority, so it is easy to inadvertently "lead" the group in a different direction as opposed to being left to its own devices. Secondly, because Judy is the manager of the group, she will throw her weight around to stay in control.

A situation like this is very damaging. The group members, thinking they are not allowed to do what they were initially promised, end up being only partially committed to the final outcome, at best. They wonder why they were brought together in the first place, and question the manager's credibility.

Credibility for a manager and a facilitator is so crucial. The group must be able to trust that you will do what you say you're going to do. In today's world, credibility is a word that gets thrown around a lot. You've heard the phrase, "Walk the talk." These are just fancy words, and sometimes detract from the real message. You can't be a strong facilitator without credibility. If you don't know the answer to something, admit it — then promise to find out the answer and communicate it. If your group is told they will be able to make a decision themselves, let them make it.

There are many facilitators who have specific opinions, but are able to withhold their comments. Consider Martin's situation.

> Martin is the facilitator for a group of plant employees. They have responsibility for scheduling maintenance for plant equipment. Martin used to maintain equipment in a previous job. Now, he is a team leader responsible for facilitating his group meetings. He has specific ideas about how equipment should be maintained, but he realizes he will need to remain silent. Without any interference from Martin, the group will be allowed to decide on a maintenance schedule and fully support the plan they've developed.

Martin understands the importance of letting a group take ownership for their decisions. He avoids stating his own opinion, concentrates on moving the group through the agenda, and allows the group to draw their own conclusions.

Content Versus Process

To be an effective facilitator, you must first understand the differences between content and process. Knowing these differences will help you guide a group through the process and do the real job of a facilitator. You will also become better at staying out of the content.

Process refers to the way the group works together. It's the methodology the group uses. Process is *how* a group accomplishes a goal. As the facilitator, you actually develop the process for the group by identifying the meeting outcome statement and writing the agenda.

For example, imagine that a group has been brought together to develop a list of materials that they'll need for the new company library. On the process side, they use methods that will help them develop the list as effectively as possible:

- Brainstorm a list of desired items.
- Clarify items on the list.
- Eliminate items from the list that the group agrees are unnecessary.

There are also process issues that involve behavior. Ground rules describe how the group will be working together, such as:

- Allow only one person to talk at a time.
- Be on time.
- Participate fully.

Content refers to the actual ideas, suggestions and decisions that come out of a group discussion. Content is *what* a group does to accomplish a goal. It is the actual subject matter, ideas and decisions made by the group.

For example, consider the group who was brought together to develop a list of materials needed for the new company library. On the content side, members begin to discuss actual items that they'd like to have in the library. Items include:

- sofa
- tables/chairs
- bookshelves
- desk
- coffee machine
- soft drink machine

Figure 2.1

Process Versus Content Table

Process the "How"	Content the "What"	Content Examples
Brainstorm a list	A specific opinion	"I prefer xyz vendor."
Clarify a list	A specific fact	"Our market share is "x."
Decide by discussing	A specific idea	"We need a TV."
Eliminate items from a list	A specific decision	"May 3rd is the deadline."
Listen effectively	A specific action	"We'll monitor revenue."
Use a facilitator		

Figure 2.1 gives you a summary of process and content. Process refers to elements that describe how a group works together to reach the intended outcome. Content refers to examples of what the group decides to do to reach an outcome.

Content Neutral and Process-Oriented

The facilitator should show neutrality on all content issues through appropriate words, body language, and voice tone. Unspoken actions can be just as important as words in displaying neutrality.

Have you ever observed a police officer who directs traffic? He or she stands in the middle of the street, telling cars when to go, stop, or turn. The officer is directing traffic, just like a facilitator directs the flow of discussion. The officer never drives anyone's car, just like the facilitator never contributes an idea to the discussion. In this way the officer and facilitator maintain neutrality. However, the officer may show his or her disapproval of a car's driving style with a scowl or frown. The facilitator could show the same type of disapproval. Both words and body language must be kept in check to maintain authentic neutrality.

The facilitator in the following examples is *not* being content neutral:

A telecommunications company has been experiencing an unusual number of outages. A group of technical support representatives is meeting to determine how to reduce these service failures. Julia, one of the TSR's makes a suggestion for Olivia, the facilitator to write on the flip chart. Olivia doesn't agree with the suggestion. After a shrug, the item is never added to the list.

Rule #1: It is not up to the facilitator to decide whether an item is worthy of consideration. The facilitator should write down all suggestions. If the group likes the ideas, then the group should be able to consider and discuss it at the appropriate point in the process — regardless of what the facilitator thinks of the idea.

A group of call center managers are meeting to decide how to handle a recent increase in call volume. They report to Tony, who also happens to be the facilitator. Tony sees the group struggling at an important decision point. He finally says, "OK, everyone. We're going to do it *this* way."

Rule #2: The facilitator should always allow the group members to make the decision, even if they have to struggle or seem uncertain. It is still the group's decision to make, even if you are both the facilitator and the boss. If they were originally given the authority to make the decision, they should be encouraged to make it.

A lumber company has been trying to increase their market share by pursuing retail businesses. The sales group has been developing a plan that lays out how retail businesses should be approached. The group reaches a consensus on the plan, but the facilitator, Vincent, does not think it will work. He says, "That's not an acceptable decision. Try something else."

Rule #3: The facilitator should live with the group's decision, whatever it is.

A group of attorneys is meeting to identify options for defending one of their clients. Andrea, an influential senior attorney, makes a suggestion. The facilitator, Michael, really likes this particular suggestion and says, "That's a great idea."

Rule #4: Even if the facilitator likes an idea, he or she should make no attempt to influence the group.

The facilitator should deal only with the meeting's process issues and be *process-oriented*. In other words, focus on *how* the group is working together. Here are some examples of what the facilitator *should* say in order to be process-oriented:

A group of programmers is meeting to decide on a new system that will be more productive and more reliable. They are very excited about the opportunity to make some significant improvements in the organization. They start making suggestions enthusiastically, but several people are talking at the same time. Tonya, the facilitator says, *"It seems that there is a lot of interrupting going on. Let's remember our ground rules and have just one person talking at a time."*

Rule #1: The facilitator is concerned with *how* the group is communicating, not the ideas being discussed. This is appropriate.

John, a service manager for a large sporting goods chain wants to make a comment about a diagram that Mary is presenting to the group. He interrupts her and causes her to lose her train of thought. Judy, the facilitator, says, *"John, could you please hold on? I'll get right back to you as soon as Mary has finished explaining this diagram."*

Rule #2: The facilitator is acting as a conductor in directing the flow of the conversation just as a conductor directs the flow of music. This provides a needed service to the meeting-goers.

A group of supervisors has just completed brainstorming a list of possible performance standards for their telemarketing representatives. It is time for the group to clarify anything on the list that is unclear. Jason (the facilitator), asks the group, *"Does anyone need clarification on these suggestions?"*

Rule #3: The facilitator is ensuring that group members understand the ideas that are listed so that they will be able to make a better decision on the value of the ideas.

Figure 2.2

Examples of Content and Process

On Remaining Content Neutral	On Being Process-Oriented
1. Accept all ideas	1. Encourage participation
2. Allow the group to make decisions	2. Ensure all ideas/statements are understood/heard
3. Live with all group decisions	3. Enforce the ground rules
4. Avoid influencing the group	4. Focus on HOW the group is communicating

Gina is facilitating her group as they identify the causes of billing errors. She begins the meeting and is in the process of reviewing the planned agenda. She says, *"I recommend we brainstorm a list."*

Rule #4: Since this suggestion focuses on a process, it is appropriate for the facilitator to make a recommendation, unless the group prefers doing something else.

Matthew is facilitating a group who is brainstorming a list of solutions for improving productivity in the key entry department. They have been brainstorming for 20 minutes and are making fewer and fewer suggestions. Matthew says, *"It seems that the flow of ideas has slowed down. Are we ready to move on to the next step?"*

Rule #5: This question keeps the group moving forward and is an appropriate statement for the facilitator to make.

Figure 2.2 describes the behaviors a facilitator exhibits for remaining content neutral and process-oriented. This accurately describes what *should* be done to focus in on the appropriate areas. Remaining content neutral means accepting group decisions ideas and input. Being process-oriented means concentrating on how the group is working together and the route that will be followed to reach the intended outcome.

The Real World

Often, the appointed meeting facilitator is interested in the content of the discussion. The group could decide something that directly impacts the facilitator. When this happens, maintain your credibility by:

- Explaining at the beginning of the meeting that you have a stake in the decision and would like to give your input on a limited basis. Make sure the group is comfortable with this.
- Acknowledging your bias by saying, "I'm stepping out of my role as facilitator to tell you that I agree with Leo's suggestion because of our deadline. Now, I'll step back into my role."
- Limiting the number of times you give your opinion to only the most important issues. If you give your own ideas as a matter of habit, the group may start to resent your involvement, thereby resisting your ideas, no matter how good they are.
- Involving yourself in the content of the meeting only to save the group unnecessary time and effort. If you know something that will help the group, share this with them: "You may want to talk to Martha Porter. I believe she worked in the technology group that developed that product. She knows a lot about it."

If you have strong opinions about the issue to be discussed, it may be best to get someone else facilitate. Then, you can contribute as a group member and will not have to worry about holding back your opinion.

Chapter Summary

The Facilitator's Greatest Skill

This chapter discusses one of the most important skills for a facilitator. When guiding the group, you must allow participants to made their own decisions. You are there to keep them organized. They must take ownership for the business issues being addressed. By focusing on process and remaining content neutral, you help them use their skills and experience to make a contribution to the organization.

What Is a Facilitator?

A facilitator is someone who helps groups work together to make decisions, develop plans, and implement those plans. The best facilitator is the person who can be neutral on the issues being discussed.

Being Process-Oriented

Process refers to *how* the group is working together. A facilitator should be process-oriented, which means pointing out ways the group can work together more effectively, developing the meeting outcome and agenda, and choosing methods such as brainstorming.

Being Content Neutral

Content refers to the actual issues discussed, or *what* the meeting must address. A facilitator should be content neutral, which means not sharing personal opinions and instead helping the group to confer and decide. If group members have authority to make a decision themselves, they begin to resent a facilitator who constantly forces his or her opinion on them. They often will give up their authority position and stop participating. Commitment and ownership disappear.

What Happens in the Real World

There are times when the facilitator wants to share his or her opinion. The facilitator can "step out of role" and state a personal opinion. This must be done after careful consideration. Do this with only the most important issues, so it doesn't become a habit. If you know something that will save the group from unnecessary work, it is also appropriate to "step out of role."

The facilitator's greatest skill is that of being content neutral. It ensures the group is fully supported yet allowed to make its best decision. Each group member feels a greater sense of ownership and therefore takes a greater interest in how to make improvements in the business.

Most organizations are concerned with how to improve performance and motivate employees. You can help make this happen by allowing your groups to use the authority they are given and do what *they* feel is best. A group of people working together to make the best decisions possible is generally better than one person directing others. When groups are truly involved, they are more willing to give their whole-hearted support, because they own their decisions and will strive to implement them successfully.

How Do I
Get Them to Talk?

Facilitator: "What would the group like to do with this item —
delete it or keep it on the list?"

Long, pregnant pause.

Facilitator: "Well, what do you think?"

Still no answer.

Facilitator: "Uh, John, what do you think?"

---

*T*here is nothing worse than standing up in front of a group and not getting a response to a question. It's amazing how warm the room suddenly becomes when this happens. As anyone who has experienced this knows, it's uncomfortable and frustrating.

Some groups are more talkative than others, but if you have the right tools, you can get the vast majority of groups active and involved in the discussion. This chapter will describe what is necessary to make this happen. Facilitating an effective discussion is possible if you utilize some important skills.

First, show you are interested in what the group members are saying by exhibiting active listening. You also model this skill for them to use with each other to ensure quality communication. Second, it is important to use questions effectively. You learn which types of questions encourage participation and develop many examples for different situations. Last, this chapter discusses how to direct the conversation flow so that participation is equalized among all group members, both the introverted and extroverted (otherwise known as the overly dominant individuals).

How important is it to get the group's wholehearted input in a discussion? As the issue discussed becomes more serious, the need for discussion is more critical. Consider the launch of the space shuttle Challenger on January 28, 1986. The mission ended 73 seconds after launch due to O-rings that did not seal in the cold temperature of thirty-six degrees Fahrenheit. The crew of seven, including the teacher Christa McAuliffe, perished in this tragic accident.

On the evening before the launch, managers and engineers held a telephone conference to discuss the concerns about whether the launch should be delayed. Personnel from Morton Thiokol, Marshall Space Flight Center, and Kennedy Space Center were present. In her book, *The Challenger Launch Decision*, Diane Vaughan indicates that Thiokol engineers were not in favor of launching because of a possible problem with the O-rings.

One wonders whether the discussion fully clarified why the engineers were concerned about the O-rings. Evidently, they did not convince others of the potential danger. This indicates the discussion was not as effective as it could have been. There were certainly other factors that also contributed to the decision to launch the Challenger. However, the decision obviously resulted in tragic consequences.

While the typical business person rarely makes life and death decisions, the need for effective discussion remains. First of all, as the facilitator, you must create the standard for effective discussion by modeling it as the group works together. When the facilitator sets the tone as an effective communicator, the group will follow suit.

Exhibiting Active Listening

Active listening is a skill you must learn in order to be an effective facilitator. Active listening encourages group members to participate. It also ensures that each participant is fully understood.

There are three steps in the active listening process:

1. Nonverbal acknowledgment: This encourages the speaker to continue, and assures the speaker that he or she is heard. Examples are head nods, eye contact, facing the speaker, and any nonverbal cue that shows the speaker that you are paying attention to the message without taking control away from the person speaking.

2. Rephrasing: This is a way to verify what the speaker said. For example, "So, are you saying ...?" Use the rephrasing technique when the speaker is saying something that might not be immediately understood by the group.

3. Empathy response: This plays back the speaker's unspoken feelings that are expressed with voice tone and body language. It is one of the best ways to calm a person who is emotional or upset. It is also a very important method for showing that you are listening and *do* understand what the speaker is saying. Examples of an empathy response are, "You seem to be satisfied with this solution according to what you're saying," or "I get the impression that you have some serious concerns about this option." Usually the empathy response invites further explanation from the speaker because it encourages the speaker (and the rest of the group) to give input.

Active listening is so important; it should be applied to every area of a person's life. It helps you understand the real meaning behind the message. People communicate using three elements: words, voice tone, and body language.

Dr. Albert Mehrabien, a UCLA psychologist, conducted research on these communication elements. He found that words constitute only seven percent of the total message. Voice tone is 38 percent of the overall message and body language (including facial expressions and gestures) is 55 percent. Since *what* a person says (the actual words) contributes to such a small part of the total message, we understand the full essence of a message by concentrating on *how* the speaker is presenting his or her message. This is done by focusing on voice tone and body language.

For example, let's say that your son comes home from school and says to you, "I'm not going back to school." If you were only concentrating on the words, or seven percent of his message, a likely response from you would be, "Oh, yes, you ARE going back to school!" Now consider the feelings behind the words, revealed by his voice tone and body language

(93 percent of the full message). Your son's downcast eyes and angry voice indicate he just had a terrible day. What is a better response? Something that showed your son you really listened to him. How about, "Sounds like you had a bad day at school. What happened?" Which response will help your son be more open to a discussion with you? Definitely, the second one!

Active listening in the work place helps you in much the same way. It gives you a better chance of really understanding a person's opinions, ideas or concerns. Also, people are more open to giving their input when they feel they're heard and understood. Through active listening, you create opportunities to address key issues that impact work performance.

In the early '70s, I worked for an Atlanta-based company called Food Giant, Inc., a grocery chain consisting of 85 stores that then had a major share of the Atlanta market. I was asked to facilitate some of the management seminars. The participants consisted of mostly male employees who managed the retail stores. The years of service for these managers ranged from 10 to 20 years. I had worked there for only a few years. It was difficult for me to "teach" these managers much of anything. They had much more experience than me; I was a recent college graduate. I quickly learned that my best chance of helping them learn the art of managing was to facilitate the discussion and *listen* to what they had to say. I could then pull together their comments and apply them to the learning points of the seminar.

To this day, I believe that I would not have been as successful in that situation if I had assumed the role of teacher, with my level of experience being so limited. Instead, my posture was that of a good listener, thus resulting in discussions that were quite valuable for all involved.

The facilitator's role includes specific active listening techniques, thus setting the tone for meeting participants to contribute openly, just as they did at Food Giant. Here are some ways to apply active listening:

- Maintain eye contact with each person who is speaking. Show you are listening with head nods, and other nonverbal cues.
- Take the input of all members seriously without discounting any suggestions. "Margaret, let's write down your suggestion so everyone can consider it."
- Encourage the group to address everyone's input in some way by asking for comments on a particular suggestion, or by boarding the comment. "Would anyone care to comment on John's recommendation?"

- Periodically summarize what was expressed by restating comments. "So far, several people have expressed their concerns about pushing back the time frame for this project."
- Point out the similarities among different comments that have been expressed at different times. "I believe this concern was also expressed earlier, when Barbara discussed the short time frame."
- Point out the deeper issues behind what is expressed by observing body language and voice tone. "It seems the group is uncomfortable about the missing information in this report, but it's difficult deciding what to do about it. What ideas do you have for finding the information?"

Using Questions Effectively

Here's an exercise for you to try. Seek out an acquaintance, someone you know, but not very well. Make a point of asking this person a series of open questions on any subject, personal or business. You will find that it is much easier to carry on a conversation, *and* control the topics discussed, through the use of questions. The term "discussion" implies that there is more than one person speaking. To prevent a discussion from turning into a monologue (one person doing all the talking), use questions.

You would use this same type of questioning technique when facilitating, only for a number of reasons other than just making conversation. Figure 3.1 describes some common instances, and also some sample questions that you can ask.

Figure 3.1

Why the Facilitator Asks Questions

Reason	Example
1. To probe for specifics	"Which date in January would you prefer?"
2. To point out something you've observed	"Have we gotten off track?"
3. To reach CLOSURE (To reach closure, get the group's agreement to move on to a new topic.)	"Are we ready to move on to the next step?"

Figure 3.1, continued

Why the Facilitator Asks Questions

Reason	Example
4. To get the group to participate	"What are your ideas?" or "What additional ideas do you have?"
5. To get the group's agreement	"Does everyone agree that we can remove this item from the list?"
6. To contract with the group	"Is everyone willing to follow these ground rules?
7. To find out why the group is stuck	"We seem to be having some difficulty coming up with ideas. Can we discuss what's causing this?"
8. To find out feelings	"What is your feeling about this?" "Are you comfortable with this?"
9. To ensure understanding	"So, are you saying that you'd prefer a less challenging goal?"

How to Ask Questions

The following suggestions will help you generate a focused discussion. First, use open-ended questions often. This enables ideas, feelings, and opinions to emerge. An open-ended question is one that requires more than two or three words to answer and more than yes or no. It can also be useful to ask closed-ended questions when you look for specific information, since a closed question encourages a specific, shorter answer, usually one to three words.

Open: "What is your opinion of ... "
Closed: "Does the group want to follow this suggestion?"

Open: "How would you like me to phrase that?"
Closed: "Is it acceptable to say ...?"

Open: "Why do you have concerns about this opinion?"
Closed: "Are you concerned about this?"

After asking a question, give plenty of time for the group to answer it. If you don't get an answer, try rephrasing your question; members may not have understood what you were asking.

First question: "What is your opinion of..."
Second question: "Are you willing to follow this suggestion?"

Note that the second question is a closed one, which is possibly another way to get participation, even if it's limited. You can always follow up with yet another question to get additional input. Just remember to ask only one question at a time rather than throwing out two questions, one after the other, without giving the group time to answer the first one.

Ask questions that help the group take action. For example, if the members are discussing whether they want to hire outside consultants to help with a portion of the project the group is working on, some questions you might want to ask are:

"Who would like to explore this option further?"
"How does the rest of the group feel about this?"

Use leading questions judiciously, as they are two-edged swords. They are questions phrased in a manner that suggests a desired answer. When such questions contain statements of opinion and begin with words like, "Don't you think ...?" or "Isn't it ...?," they manipulate the listener into agreeing with the speaker or following the speaker's suggestions.

"Don't you think we should create a new list?"
"Isn't it going to be difficult to follow that through to completion?"

However, subtle leading questions can be effective in helping a group reach consensus by establishing positive feedback.

"Can I assume that everyone agrees to the first phase of this plan?"

Once a question is answered, accept all answers. The facilitator accepts answers 100 percent of the time. It is up to the group to decide the value of the input. The facilitator is there to make it easy for everyone's input to be heard and considered.

Directing the Conversation Flow

Directing the conversation flow means establishing a balance of participation among all group members. This results in a smooth flow of information passing from one group member to another. The group is then more productive and more organized in approaching its work. Directing the conversation flow effectively helps manage those individuals who tend to dominate the discussion. You can get more participation from those individuals who tend towards silence.

Here are some methods that will help you direct the conversation flow. First of all, seek equal involvement. Strive to get everyone to give input without putting anyone on the "hot seat." In other words, avoid putting someone in an awkward position by calling on him or her and expecting an immediate answer. Call on people by name only as a follow up option. First, try encouraging participation from all.

> "It's important to get as many ideas as possible. If yours is not represented on the flip chart, let us know."

> "Let's get everyone's input on this. Joe, have you had a chance to form an opinion at this point?"

Always discourage people from interrupting each other. Remind the group of the importance of listening to each idea, one at a time, in order to fully understand what is being said. Also, if *sidebar conversations* occur, when two or more people break off from the rest of the group for a private discussion, remind the group to listen to the person who currently has the floor.

> "Let's all focus on what Mary is saying."

> "Let's remember our ground rule of only one person talking at a time."

> "It's difficult for some to hear or stay focused with other discussions going on. Please hold your discussion until Maria finishes and then we'll hear from someone else."

There is one situation when *polite* interrupting is appropriate. This occurs when you are working with extremely vocal group members who contribute with a lot of detail. It is difficult for anyone; including you, the facilitator, to find a break in the conversation in order to contribute to this type of discussion. In order to create an opening in the discussion for yourself or for some other eager group member, listen carefully to the person who has the floor. You can tell when this group member is about to deliver the last word of his or her message. Interrupt the last word being delivered, by saying something like, "Jacob is next." This is also your opportunity to address the group.

It is critical that all members have an opportunity to voice their ideas, suggestions, and concerns. As a facilitator, you do this by acknowledging someone who was trying to give his or her input; promise to come back to that person at the next opportunity.

"I saw Paul's hand first, but I'll come back to Richard next."

If you have ever been hesitant to make a suggestion or comment during a meeting, then you know how important it is to give all an opportunity to speak. The facilitator can make a difference in creating an atmosphere where it is safe for all to contribute.

A facilitator also needs to be proficient at writing the group's suggestions and ideas on a flip chart. Writing down ideas helps keep the flow of conversation more orderly. It isn't always necessary to log everything that is said. If you are not sure, ask the group if it is ready to list ideas and suggestions on the flip chart.

The Flip Chart

Several types of visual aides can be used in facilitating a meeting, but the flip chart is the most useful. It is preferred because you can build a list while the group is contributing ideas. As each sheet fills up, you can tear it off and hang it up with masking tape for the group's continued reference. To use the flip chart effectively, keep in mind the following points:

- Make sure you have plenty of paper and different colored markers before the meeting starts, so there will be no delays once the session begins.
- Use group members' exact words when boarding suggestions or ideas. If there is not enough room to use the exact words, ask the contributor of the idea, "What should I write down?"
- As you are writing down each idea, use two different colored markers and alternate the colors. This technique makes it easier to read the ideas. Examples are blue and green, or light blue and dark blue. Avoid bright colors such as red, yellow or orange which are more difficult to read. However, since red is emotionally charged, it can be used to highlight important areas.

- Make changes to the original list. Once a list has been built and the group is ready to eliminate or clarify items, write down the clarification next to the corresponding idea, or draw a line through a discarded idea on the original list. Rewriting the list takes time and the group could get impatient.
- Keep all flip chart sheets within view of all group members' for easy reference.

Signs of Good Communication

Practicing these guidelines for good communication certainly makes a positive impact on how your groups are interacting. However, there is no guarantee that things will go smoothly.

A couple of years ago, I facilitated a group of researchers and engineers in a large experimental facility. They were meeting to improve some of their methods and procedures. I was scheduled to spend the entire day with them, so I did some icebreaker activities with them. They were designed to increase the group's comfort level with each other and with myself.

As the morning wore on, I noticed the tension in the air. Group members did not participate. I also noticed they did not make eye contact with me. I knew there was something wrong. I tactfully mentioned that there wasn't much participation. Then, I asked if there was something I could do to get the group more involved. I didn't get much of a response, so I called a break and asked the same question to someone who had been more vocal during the session.

He told me that I insulted the group by beginning the session with the icebreaker activities. They also had some expectations that I had not bothered to find out. I had originally interviewed their manager one month before the session, but had not spoken to any group members.

Getting this feedback was not very much fun, but *not* getting it would have been even worse. At least now, I could try to correct the situation. When we started back, I apologized for my "bad start," and asked a few more questions to find out what the group needed from me. I gave them a chance to voice their concerns and used empathy, even when they gave me feedback on my own mistakes. The session turned out to be a great success, even after starting out in a "ditch." Subsequently, they asked me to facilitate three additional sessions for that group.

When the meeting is not going well, how can you tell? First of all, you must be aware of any restlessness. This is when members are shifting in their seats, or engaged in outside activities (such as reading or writing). The group may need a break, or there could be something else bothering them. You have to notice these signals occurring first; only then, will you have an opportunity to do something.

Another sign to be aware of is when the group does not participate, or when uncomfortable silences occur. This happens for a number of reasons and is usually coupled with people avoiding eye contact with you or each other. Body language and facial expressions say a lot about how a group is feeling. The group could be unhappy with you or with someone else, or they may not like the particular topic of discussion. First you must notice there is something wrong because group members won't always tell you. After you observe it, then you can call a break and talk to someone privately or tactfully ask the group as a whole.

What are the signs that the meeting is going well? You'll usually notice more excitement and enthusiasm from the group members. They are generally willing to accept input from each other and are able to interact openly to understand the different perspectives. People are willing to participate and are fully engaged in the discussion. They take the time to listen and understand what is being said. There is also more tolerance for individual differences in opinion. The atmosphere is comfortable, full of energy but not tense. This is the type of meeting environment that all facilitators strive for and enjoy.

Chapter Summary

The Importance of Communication

As human beings, we communicate in many different ways, even when we are not aware that we are sending messages. The quality of our communication affects us in every area of our lives: with our business associates, friends, acquaintances, and most importantly, the people we love. The manner in which we communicate with others almost always sets the tone for how others communicate back to us. If we concentrate on improving the quality of our communication, everyone will gain a greater understanding of what we want to say. This "connection" surely enhances and improves our ability to work together in accomplishing those goals that are most important to us.

Exhibit Active Listening

Active listening occurs by observing the words, voice tone and body language. This helps ensure understanding and models how group members should be communicating with each other. Remember to maintain eye contact, treat all input seriously, summarize points made during the discussion and highlight similarities among ideas and deeper issues.

Use Questions Effectively

Effective questions help the facilitator probe for more information, point out his or her own observations, reach closure, encourage participation, verify agreement, and contract with the group. When asking questions, remember to use open questions and give the group time to answer the question. You can also ask questions that help the group take action. Remember, a facilitator accepts all answers. This practice encourages participation.

Closed questions are also helpful when used in conjunction with open questions. They help get specific, shorter answers when focusing on an issue or decision point.

Directing the Conversation Flow

The conversation should be balanced within the group by seeking equal involvement, discouraging interruptions, giving everyone an opportunity to speak and writing down all suggestions on the flip chart.

The Flip Chart

The flip chart is the best tool for recording group member's input and then posting the flip chart sheets for everyone to see. Remember to have plenty of flip chart pads, markers and masking tape on hand. Write down the exact words of the group members and make changes to the original list, rather than starting a new list when a change is made.

Signs of Good Communication

Observe the verbal and nonverbal cues to determine how the meeting is going and whether the group members are satisfied with its progress. Body language and voice tone will often indicate members' thoughts and feelings more accurately than spoken words.

Using the principles suggested in this chapter will ensure you never have to wonder how to get your group members talking. Your groups will be comfortable participating and will learn to respect each other's input as well. A comfortable environment creates a group that is more open, more accepting and more willing to become fully engaged in the business of the meeting.

The Art of Facilitation

Tim: "Where were we?"

Kevin: "I don't know, I lost track."

Tim: "Why can't we ever have a meeting without getting off the subject?"

Kevin: "Well, what *is* the subject?"

You may not have expressed these sentiments, but most people have experienced them. It's challenging to contribute one's ideas in a meeting and try to keep everyone on topic at the same time. As a facilitator, your role is to keenly observe what is happening to make sure that the group is following the agenda. You must also monitor the group's behavior to ensure members are working together as effectively as possible.

Have you ever observed the world from an airplane window? Or looked down from the top floor of a tall building? Or viewed a peaceful valley from the top of a mountain? These activities give a perspective that you don't get when both feet are on the ground. It is easier to notice things from a distance when you are removed from the situation. When you are dealing with a tough issue, and you go to a friend for advice, you are doing the same thing: seeking objectivity. You want to find someone who can listen and respond objectively.

As a facilitator, it is this kind of objectivity that enables you to identify potential problems like those Tim and Kevin are facing. You can then help the group avoid or work through these obstacles. You must stay out of the content of the group's discussion and not exhibit any bias about the project the group is assigned. This objectivity will help you approach the group with a "bird's eye view." You need to mentally take a step away from the group and analyze what is happening.

This chapter will describe how you can objectively monitor a group's progress toward its objectives. There are four competencies. The first one is keeping the group aware. The group needs help in becoming conscious about how well they are progressing. The next competency is building consensus — the best method for group decision making. Maintaining flexibility and displaying tactfulness are two other skills that reflect an awareness of the group's needs and sensitivities, and the willingness to accommodate them.

To be competent in these areas, you must be able to mentally remove yourself from the situation and objectively assess what is happening among the individuals in the room. You are actually doing two things at once. First, you facilitate the meeting by asking questions, listening, and leading the group through the steps in the agenda. Secondly, you observe how members of the group work together, and constantly look for ways they can work together more effectively. This activity is called *parallel processing*.

Keeping the Group Aware

As a facilitator, you keep the group informed and aware of all pertinent information at all times. This includes reminding the group of the desired outcome, topic for discussion, methods for working together or anything else that is helpful. A group can easily get off track. You can be very useful in preventing this.

You become a camera for the group. You record what you're seeing, and play back by verbalizing your observations. Real video recording is quite valuable. I use it for a presentation skills workshop. Participants deliver their prepared presentations to the group while the camera records the speech. Then I rewind the tape and play it back to the group. The speaker sees exactly how he or she delivered the presentation and is able to pinpoint areas of strength and areas for improvement. You can provide the same service as the camera and VCR.

Keep the group aware by being *transparent*: candidly express your observations about what the group is doing and how members are working together. This means you'll need to monitor two main areas, what the group is working on (the tasks), and how well members are working together (the behaviors).

Constant reference to the agenda will help you concentrate on what tasks the group *should* be working on. Then you can compare this to the tasks members are *actually* working on. For example, I was recently working with a group of senior level managers in a long distance company. They had just brainstormed a list of solutions for improving their product roll-out procedures. The agenda indicated they should clarify any solutions that were unclear. However, several of the managers began assessing which solutions would work and which ones would not work. My role, as facilitator, was to point that out by saying something like, "I'm noticing that we have moved into evaluating these solutions, but I don't think we've finished clarifying them yet. Let's make sure we've finished the clarification process first so that when we evaluate, we will understand what we are evaluating."

Always start out with a description of what is actually happening. Then explain why this is not desirable. It may also be helpful to describe what should be done to correct the situation or ask the group for their ideas. If you observe the group doing something especially well, remember to point this out also.

Another area to monitor is group members' behavior. This will help you focus on how well they are working together. A key area to concentrate on is whether group members are following the ground rules. I was facilitating a group of managers who worked for a cable company. We were having ongoing meetings to make improvements in their internal methods and procedures. One of the ground rules was to be on time. The first few times people came in late to our meetings, I overlooked it. But, I quickly realized that tardiness was becoming a pattern. So, I said, "One of our ground rules is to be on time. I'm noticing this is not always happening. What can we do to make sure people arrive on time, so we can begin our meetings on schedule?" By pointing this out, and asking for their ideas on how to correct the situation, the group was able to address it and minimize the problem.

When to Keep the Group Aware

There are several specific tasks and behaviors you should monitor to keep group members aware. Don't limit yourself to only these examples. They are just a few of the most important areas in which to focus your attention.

- *Outcome*: When the group gets bogged down in irrelevant discussion, it is helpful to remind group members of the intended meeting outcome: "Let's remember, we have to ultimately end up with five recommendations."
- *Time frame*: Meeting participants can easily lose track of time. It is important that meetings start and end on time unless the group agrees to extend or make a change in the time. The facilitator can issue reminders: "We have 30 minutes left. Do you want to continue clarifying these ideas, or are you ready to start narrowing down the list?"
- *Group agreements/decisions*: Remind the group what members have already agreed upon. This sometimes helps them make future decisions: "You've already agreed to do the training in-house. What's next?"
- *Group accomplishments or progress*: Note the progress of the group as it relates to the planned agenda or time line for its project: "We are currently on step five in the agenda and are now ready to go to step six," or "You've now established the true cause of the problem and are ready to identify possible solutions."
- *Staying on track*: Make the group aware when it begins discussing a topic that isn't on the agenda: "Let's remember, we're here to discuss employee complaints, not whether we need to hire more employees. Would you like to put the subject of hiring on our parking lot?"

A *parking lot* is a tool I use whenever I facilitate. It is a posted easel sheet entitled "Parking Lot" at the top. It is used to write down important topics that are not part of the current meeting agenda that the group may want to address later. Make sure that all parking lot issues are addressed at some point, or that there is group agreement on how those issues will be addressed.

Meeting participants need reminding in order to stay on track. Just as you might refer to a road map when you are driving to a new destination, use the agenda as a guide and refer to it often: "Now, to summarize, we're discussing ... so that we can ...."

- *Group effectiveness*: Look for ways to compliment the group — not on the quality of its ideas, decisions or plans, but on its effectiveness in working together. This will help ensure your neutrality on content: "We had to work out some challenges in the beginning, but you seem to be progressing very nicely as a unified group."

- *Ground rules*: It is sometimes necessary to remind the group of the ground rules: "One of the ground rules is to avoid interrupting one another. Even though you are enthusiastic about this issue, try to have only one person talking at a time."
- *Background information or parameters*: There are areas not specifically listed on the agenda that need clarification from the group. A group has certain parameters that it is operating under; such as a budget, time frame, and limits of authority. Any background information surrounding the meeting agenda is probably helpful: "Please remember that we have a headcount limit of no more than five additional new-hires. This was announced during the conference last month." By keeping the group aware of what is happening, not just inside the meeting, but outside the meeting, you become a valuable asset.

Building Group Consensus

Consensus, or agreement, should occur whenever the group needs commitment from all members on a particular decision or course of action. A good working definition for consensus is a decision made by the group that all members can support. It is not necessary to have 100 percent agreement on a decision in order to have a consensus. Consensus calls for all group members to support the decision 100 percent, not necessarily agree 100 percent. It is important that the group has a clear understanding of what consensus means in order to effectively reach a consensus.

Importance of Consensus Versus Other Types of Decision Making

There are other types of decision making in addition to consensus. They are unanimity, majority vote, and compromise.

Often groups confuse consensus with unanimity, in which each group member agrees with the decision 100 percent. One story that supports the value of consensus instead of unanimity is the Cuban Missile Crisis. Robert Kennedy, in his memoir of the Cuban Missile Crisis, *Thirteen Days*, describes how a committee of chosen government officials worked together in making recommendations to President John F. Kennedy on how to handle the crisis.

Kennedy says that it was very important for the President to get a variety of ideas and opinions achieved through discussion and debate. Unanimity, in which everyone agrees on the issues, creates potential for making a mediocre decision.

Relying on majority vote is another pitfall for groups. People tend to resort to this easy way out when they must select one option out of several choices. Someone usually says, "Let's vote on it." Voting ensures that someone loses out, with no chance to discuss his or her views. Voting tends to eliminate discussion, and severely limits the level of commitment in support of the final decision. When is it appropriate to vote? When the group is considering many options (six or more) and members want to narrow the list down to a few options (two or three) for further discussion. After the list is narrowed, the group should discuss where the members stand with each option, striving to reach a consensus at this point.

Compromising is a settlement between two sides, with each side making some sort of concession or giving up something. Compromising should be discouraged, because it is a win/lose proposition. Each side wins something and each side also loses something. Compromise and consensus are similar, except that compromise tends to encourage limited support, since everyone has to give something up. On the other hand, consensus is a decision that each group member can fully support, because it is a win/win proposition. The decision, while not perfect for everyone, is one in which no one loses.

Here is an example that shows the difference between compromise and consensus. Most business people are involved in office moves at one time or another. This can result in a major turf war. Imagine that your company was moving to a brand new location in a brand new building and will occupy the fourth and fifth floors. The fourth floor has a beautiful view and lots of windows. The fifth floor is mostly walls. Further imagine that there are a limited number of receptionists to be assigned for each department. This could be the start of World War III!

Of course, everyone wants to be on the fourth floor and each department will want a receptionist. But someone must move to the fifth floor and some departments will not receive a receptionist. An example of a compromise would be if each department either received a fourth floor assignment *or* a receptionist, but not both. In this case each department is gaining something and giving up something. There is a lot of bargaining going on.

An example of reaching a consensus is looking at it a different way. Make the fifth floor furnishings and decor extremely appealing. Build some very nice conference rooms and break rooms. Position departments so that they share receptionists. This is a decision in which everyone benefits without having to give up too much.

It seems that sharing a receptionist sounds like a compromise. That may be true. Remember, consensus is similar to compromise. But considering what each department gets in this situation, it's clear that the consensus situation is much better for everyone than the compromise situation. Generally speaking, consensus is almost always better than compromise.

In fact, consensus is better than all other types of decision making if you are looking for the group to make a sound decision and then support that decision. Consensus allows groups to hear different perspectives and points of view. By doing so, each group member is satisfied that his or her opinion has been heard even if the group chooses not to follow an individual's suggested course of action. This creates an environment where all group members openly discuss the options and are open to supporting the overall group decision. The group may not agree with the final decision, but they are willing to support the decision. In addition, people are typically not forced to give up something they really want. People tend to look for a way that satisfies everyone's interests.

Figure 4.1 gives the highlights for each of the types of decision making. After reviewing this chart, it will be clear how consensus works compared

Figure 4.1

Types of Decision Making

	Consensus	Unanimity	Majority Vote	Compromise
Definition	100% support	100% agreement	51% wins	Halfway point for all
Pro's	All members will support	All members will support	Majority will support	All will support partially
Con's	Time consuming	Unrealistic	Creates win/lose scenario	Creates win/lose scenario
When to use	Support is needed	Clear cut issues	To narrow a list	Need breakthrough
When not to use	Short time frame	Complex issues	To make final decision	Support is needed

to the other types of decision making. Consensus is the most realistic and it creates the best scenario for group members and the organization.

How to Build Consensus

Constantly look for ways to help the group reach agreement. Consensus starts with getting agreement on the ground rules at the beginning of the session. This allows the group to agree on how it will work together and sets a consensus-building precedent.

During the rest of the meeting, look for ways to continue to build consensus. Keep a constant watch over each individual group member. Look for any signal that someone is not comfortable with the way the group is progressing. Signals might include words or actions. Look for a facial expression that shows confusion or concern. Watch for nonverbal signals — an individual may be hesitant without expressing it. If someone indicates that he or she isn't comfortable, check it out to ensure consensus: "Joan, you seem hesitant about committing to this. What do you think about this option?"

Once you've discovered that someone isn't comfortable with a proposed option, help that person explain *why* to the rest of the group. Then ask the group to develop an idea that would be acceptable to all: "So, Joan isn't comfortable with the time frame — it's too long. Has anyone else considered this?" "So, the time frame might be a problem. What ideas do you have that can be supported by everyone?"

If a group reaches consensus too quickly, be suspicious and make sure that a portion of the group hasn't decided to stop participating. If the decision is an important one, or if it has a significant impact, it is normal for the group to struggle in its course toward consensus. You might say: "Now, I expected you to discuss this issue a little more. I want to make sure that everyone is truly comfortable with this decision. Are you?"

Encourage the group to consider all views and look for ways to reach consensus. The main function of the facilitator is to ensure that people express their opinions. This helps the group hear and understand all views: "So, Al, explain your reasons for recommending this option."

Ask if the group is willing to support the proposed decision or option when the group is close to reaching a decision. This builds agreement and shows whether everyone is drawing the same conclusion: "Is everyone willing to support this so far?"

What to Do When the Group Gets Stuck

If the group is still struggling to reach a consensus, there are some additional techniques to use. First, you could try encouraging different factions to reverse roles. This sometimes helps people to understand opposing viewpoints: "John, if you were Mary, how would you feel? And Mary, how would you feel if you were John?"

It may be helpful to call a break. Sometimes, this helps as people can think about an issue for a few minutes, giving them a way to calm down if tempers have flared. If people can take some time in quiet thought, the issue may not seem as serious. Often people will even use the break time to work out their differences privately.

You can help the group by reinforcing the importance of examining all sides of an issue. Remind the group that it is healthy to disagree: "It's good that we have some disagreement on this issue. It's an important issue, so we need to consider all sides." "What specifically are you concerned about?" "Is there something you absolutely can't live with or support?"

You can also elevate the issue. This means you suggest the group consider an outside perspective or broader issue: "What have other departments done to reinforce this training?" "How would you advise someone to save money with their own personal income? This might help give you some ideas about the departmental budget cuts." This helps a group get ideas from other situations that were successful.

When to Build Consensus

A group should begin reaching consensus when smaller issues arise. This will get them moving in an agreed upon direction. It sets the tone and prepares them for the more important issues concerning consensus. You can help a group do this at several points during a meeting.

You can use the flip chart to build consensus by getting everyone's agreement before making any changes to any boarded items. "John has suggested that we remove Greenville from the list. Does everyone agree?" Any time a group member makes a suggestion to remove an item from a list, make sure the rest of the group is in agreement. You wouldn't get agreement when adding an idea to a list, or when clarifying an idea. However, once you begin narrowing down a list, group consensus is important.

Group consensus is also important when helping a group reach closure. While working in one step of the process, ask if the group is ready to move to the next step either in the process or on the agenda. "Are you ready to start evaluating these ideas, or do you need clarification on any others?" This gives members one last opportunity to contribute to the current step in the agenda before moving on. It also points out where the group currently is according to the agenda.

When it's time to clarify the outcome and present the agenda, you help a group reach consensus. Ask for clarification on the desired outcome at the beginning of the meeting. "What questions do you have about the outcome? Does everyone understand it?" Ensure the group understands the planned agenda, after pointing out each agenda item. "Does everyone understand this agenda?" You are not at the agreement phase on the outcome and agenda yet. However, if group members understand the result they want to achieve and how they'll get there by the end of the meeting, it is easier to avoid confusion and reach consensus.

There is another area where you do not get group agreement; it's on process tools. A process tool is a structured method that guides a group toward its goal, such as brainstorming. You should simply recommend the process tools you selected and listed on the agenda. You say, "I recommend we make a list, and then clarify the ideas." I have seen facilitators say, "What would you prefer doing, brainstorming or some other method?" When group members are given a choice on which methods to use, they tend to agonize. This wastes a great deal of time and group energy. Why allow a group to disagree on such minute issues? You can help them focus on the real issues of the meeting by choosing the process tools you feel are best. Focus the group's attention on *content*, not *process*. This minimizes the potential for confusion and ultimately makes it easier for the group members to reach a consensus.

There is one exception, though. If the group wants to use a method that you didn't plan for, be flexible to their needs. "I've planned to use a flow chart, but you want to brainstorm a list first. Since the group is in agreement on this, then we'll begin by brainstorming." The group is your customer. You plan for what you think is best, but always remain flexible to their needs.

Once the group makes a decision, you should always ensure that there is a true consensus. In other words, when the group makes a decision or commitment, be sure all group members can support the decision. "Is everyone willing to support this decision? John, we haven't heard from you yet — are you comfortable supporting this?" This gives everyone an opportunity to voice their concerns, if there are any.

Maintaining Sensitivity and Flexibility

You should maintain both sensitivity and flexibility in helping the group perform its work. *Sensitivity* involves protecting the self-esteem of individuals. *Flexibility* refers to the facilitator's ability to make changes based upon the group's need or request. An example of this was in the previous section; you should plan to use certain methods listed in the meeting agenda, but be flexible if the group chooses another method. There are more specific ways in which you can display sensitivity and flexibility to both help the group and set an example for how group members should treat each other:

- Foster respect for the individual. "So, from your perspective, Sue, you feel that this guideline is unfair?" Different perspectives are acceptable and desirable.
- Protect individuals from personal attack. "John, you may disagree with Tim's viewpoint, but let's refrain from personal attacks." Don't allow name-calling or insults to enter the picture.
- Encourage a climate of acceptance. "Based upon June's suggestion, it looks as though the group has yet another idea to consider." Encourage the group to consider new ideas and understand them before judging them.
- Observe what the group is doing. "It looks like we need a break." Watch for a drop in attention, shrugging of the shoulders, frowns, waning interest, tiredness, or participants avoiding eye contact.
- Project patience. "Let's review the time frames we've committed to so we can clear up some of the confusion." Be calm through any difficulties, such as delays or problems.
- Adapt to the group's needs. "Since the group prefers discussing this issue first, that's what we'll do."
- Use the group's language. Always speak and write in terms of the exact wording used by group members.
- Reinforce members' participation. Don't praise group members for coming up with a good idea, but just for their involvement. "It's great to see everyone involved — keep it up!"
- Help those with unique needs. If a group member has an individual or unique need, strive to help out. "Lynn, I know you prefer this in writing, so I'll make arrangements to have this done for you."

- Make requested changes. Make changes in the agenda based upon the group's request or need. As the facilitator, you make process recommendations, but the group ultimately decides whether it will follow your recommendations.

There is one group I facilitate that often requires flexibility on my part. There is often a change in the location or time of our planned session. Sometimes, I get there and find out the room isn't set up for the meeting or there are not enough markers for the flip chart. I always arrive early and am prepared with extra markers, flip chart pads, and masking tape. I also make sure I have plenty of patience because things don't always go perfectly. One reason this group calls me so consistently is because I am flexible and willing to make last minute changes for them.

Displaying Tactfulness

Tact is defined as the ability to deal with people without offending. You must be able to control the discussion and still remain neutral in your approach. Sometimes it is necessary to enforce a rule, or make suggestions. It is important to do these things in the most positive way possible so as not to alienate anyone. For example, if a group member gets defensive when you remind him of a ground rule he is breaking, then a chance for helping the group function more effectively is lost. Therefore, tactfulness can minimize the defensiveness that sometimes materializes when you have to enforce the rules.

Here are a few ways to be tactful:

- Think before you speak. Consider the possible impact of your words on an individual or the group as you formulate your thoughts.
- Be clear about what you're saying. Be open and direct — but never hurtful. "We've discussed how interrupting can be destructive. Yet it seems to be something that's difficult to avoid. What can I do to help?"
- Express your observations with humility. Be careful to qualify them as your opinion, using a phrase like "It seems to me that..." to preface your comments.
- Avoid blurting out what you want to say. "Hold on! We're going to be here all day at this rate!" Outbursts like this will alienate participants.

Here are some of the many different situations that call for tactfulness.

- When you need to enforce group rules or group commitments. "Bill, remember that we decided not to use acronyms anymore."
- To help the group adhere to proper procedures. "Now, group, let's not worry about whether we agree with any of these ideas. We've agreed to list them first, then discuss their value."
- To give feedback on the group's behavior. "It seems that there is a lot of sarcasm when dealing with this subject. Why?"
- To give direction and guidance to the group. "Could you summarize what you just said in a few words?"

Chapter Summary

The Group Needs You

This chapter has outlined four key ways to provide the bird's eye view so that you can help group members improve the way they work together and progress toward their stated objective. The group is counting on you to effectively use these four competencies summarized below.

Keeping the Group Aware

The group needs to be kept aware of the stated outcome, time frame, decisions made, progress made, group effectiveness, ground rules, and any other pertinent information. This is accomplished by verbalizing and pointing out observations to the group.

Building Group Consensus

Consensus is the best type of decision making for group process. The definition of consensus is a decision made by the group that all members may not agree with 100 percent, but can support 100 percent. Majority voting is only effective when the group has a long list of options and must narrow it down to a smaller, more manageable list. Voting should not be used to make a final decision regarding the one best option.

Maintaining Sensitivity and Flexibility

Sensitivity and flexibility help foster respect, protect individuals from personal attack, encourage a climate of acceptance, project patience, and adapt to the group's needs and language. A good facilitator knows that he or she exists to serve the group and help its members reach their objectives. This requires adaptability.

Displaying Tactfulness

Facilitators demonstrate tactfulness by thinking before they speak, and by expressing their thoughts clearly but with humility. The facilitator must be assertive but use tactfulness when enforcing ground rules, maintaining adherence to procedures, and giving feedback and direction.

The group needs your objectivity, and is counting on you to apply the bird's eye view to the total picture of the meeting, so that members concentrate on voicing their ideas, making decisions, and reaching their desired outcome. You must keep the discussion going, monitor what is happening, and structure the group's approach. This juggling of different skills on your part is challenging, but when done appropriately, is much appreciated by the group.

CHAPTER

5

Let's Agree
to Disagree

Every time Antonio makes a suggestion, the rest of the team
ignores it! How can we complain about his lack of commitment
when we never give him an opportunity to really be heard? And
we cut people off like this, all the time!

ᴉese comments came from a group of engineers I facilitated from a
minent organization in Atlanta. They experienced difficulty communi-
ng with each other. Some of the more introverted group members were
rrupted by others when discussing their views. Although the state-
ᴉt indicated there was trouble among group members, the group was
ᴇ to address this difficulty after one person pointed it out.
agreement and conflict can be one of the most frustrating experiences
the group and the facilitator. But, it can also be rewarding if handled
ropriately and skillfully.

; chapter will explain what conflict is, how groups typically approach
flict, and effective methods for dealing with it. You will learn tech-
ᴉes for creating open discussions around areas of disagreement. As a
ᴉlt, group members will reach solid agreement, quickly and decisively.

ᴦ personal attitude toward conflict has an impact on how the group
ᴇeives it. Conflict is normal and even necessary for a group to work

57

together effectively. Its presence ensures that different options and views are fully explored. This is critical in making a sound decision. Conflict in and of itself isn't bad; it's how conflict is handled that can be bad.

When there are problems, it's important to get the group to surface their issues. Only then can these problems be worked out. The group of engineers I facilitated had problems in how members communicated with each other. Most members felt there was very little listening taking place and quite a bit of everyone talking at the same time. Resentment started building.

As their facilitator, I helped this group by doing two things. First, I suggested they discuss their sources of disagreement. They were comfortable doing this openly and honestly. After some in-depth discussion, they concluded that there was a serious lack of listening. Second, I asked the group to identify what could be done to improve in this area. They identified some specific new behaviors that would help them improve their listening. The conflict was resolved constructively and the group became more cohesive and worked together more effectively as a result.

This is the type of resolution that all facilitators should strive for with their groups. Perfection is never possible, but getting close to perfection as is realistically possible should be the goal.

What Is Conflict?

Conflict is a disagreement within the group that is significant enough to slow down or halt the group's progress. There are three types of conflict: process conflict, content conflict and communication-style conflict.

Process conflict occurs whenever group members have trouble agreeing on *how* to go about reaching their desired outcome. Often this is centered around the use of process tools. Other process conflict can stem from disagreements over things like how often the group should meet or how the group will make decisions.

One way you can head off process conflict is by deciding ahead of time which process tools will be used, and making that recommendation. It is best not to give the group too many options when it comes to process. Simply make your recommendation; it is well within the facilitator's responsibility to select which process tools will be used. Of course, if the group has another preference, you should be flexible and use the tools preferred by the group. But ordinarily, the facilitator chooses process tools.

Content conflict occurs when the group cannot reach a consensus on ideas, alternatives, goals, outcomes, and any business issues that require agreement. When the group is deciding important issues, there are often different perspectives and different viewpoints. Content conflict can erupt over:

- choosing one option from many options;
- dealing with budget issues;
- establishing a goal;
- determining action items needed in an action plan;
- reaching a consensus on time frames and deadlines;
- targeting factors that are contributing most to a specific problem.

Content conflict is resolved by discussing the points of contention and then finding a solution that benefits all. You accomplish this by asking questions and guiding the group. As you read the rest of this chapter, you'll find many ways to help a group overcome content conflict, which is the most desirable type of conflict, since it makes it possible for the group to consider all views before making a decision.

Communication-style conflict occurs when there is a diverse mix of group members — and a diverse mix of preferred communication styles. An extroverted person might be perceived by some group members as too talkative, while an introverted person may be perceived as too quiet. Some people like to make decisions quickly and might become frustrated when someone who is analytical takes more time to make a decision. Yet, if most group members are analytical, they may resent being pressed to make a decision by a decisive person. Style differences create a potential for conflict.

While "style" should not enter into decision making, it is challenging for group members to make decisions on the value of the ideas alone, not on the potentially negative or positive perception of the person presenting the ideas. It is up to the facilitator to recognize this and assist group members in considering all options objectively while they respect each other's differences.

Whenever working with a group, look for balance. Group members should complement each other by having a variety of strengths among the individuals in the group. For example, I am a person who can make decisions quickly. This is good because I usually recognize what's important immediately, but I'm not good at considering the details. I tend to make the best decisions when I am working with someone who is more detail-oriented and forces me to slow down to consider all the facts before deciding. Groups need this same kind of balance. If all group members think the same way, why would you need a group?

How Groups Respond to Conflict

There are generally three different ways in which a group will respond to conflict:

1. healthy conflict
2. submerged conflict
3. chaotic conflict

Healthy conflict is the type of conflict illustrated at the beginning of this chapter. The group was able to identify its poor listening habits by being open and honest. They then identified how to make improvements. All groups should strive to address conflict in this manner. In this setting, people are comfortable disagreeing with each other. In fact, disagreement is viewed as a necessary and helpful element. While tempers flare at times, the conflict is almost always resolved and the group progresses comfortably. There are no hard feelings because members respect one another's differences. They have a strong level of loyalty to one another and to the commitments they made. Consequently, the group is able to accomplish its goals and perform at an extremely high level. The group described at the beginning of this chapter exceled by addressing conflict in this way.

Figure 5.1 illustrates the three responses to conflict. Healthy conflict is in the middle of the spectrum of conflict, with "submerged conflict" and "chaotic conflict" on either end.

A group that submerges conflict is very challenging for a facilitator to manage. *Submerged conflict* occurs when group members are reluctant to bring up controversial issues. They never argue because they are uncomfortable with conflict. They tend to reach consensus very quickly, with little discussion. There can be much unspoken resentment and irritation under the surface, however. This plays itself out when group members

Figure 5.1

How Groups Respond to Conflict

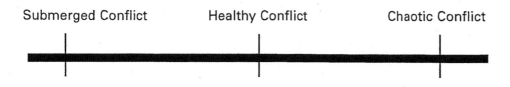

criticize the group outside the meetings. Group commitment and loyalty are low, with progress slow and goals not achieved.

Submerged conflict is sometimes the most challenging situation for the facilitator because group members refuse to discuss their differences. They prefer to "let sleeping dogs lie," so the problems fester and grow. Sadly, the group's true potential is never fully realized. Since members feel that being open is too risky, they convince themselves that the current level of performance is good enough.

One group that I worked with was so afraid of being open about their problems that their meetings had many awkward silences. No one wanted to admit that they felt manipulated and intimidated by their manager. Yet, outside of their meetings they came to me one-by-one and discussed their issues in private. Since I was the designated facilitator, I was able to listen to each individual's issues and afterwards, sit down with their manager to gently discuss what I had learned. Since he was not given the names, he was able to focus on the issues along with my recommendations.

Here are some additional ideas for helping a group move from submerged conflict to healthy conflict:

- Point out the specific behaviors that characterize submerged conflict and explain why they are not effective. "You seem to have reached this important decision quickly. I'm concerned that there may be some unspoken reservations that will compromise support for this decision." "There doesn't seem to be anyone who is willing to play devil's advocate when we reach a decision point. Are you sure you are considering all the issues thoroughly?"

- Encourage the group to discuss the issues openly and to find areas for disagreement. Remind them that disagreement is healthy and will assist them in making better decisions because they have considered all areas of concern.
- If necessary, speak with some of the group members individually to encourage them to be more open.

Groups that handle *conflict chaotically* are challenging. Unlike submerged groups, chaotic groups are so comfortable with conflict that members argue excessively. The good news is that a chaotic group is generally open, so you can recognize their chaotic approach; but resolution to disagreement is rarely reached. Group members are sometimes loud during their discussions, with a lot of interrupting. Sometimes sarcastic humor runs rampant, and it inflicts pain on the self-esteem of group members. With such an abundance of energy, the group has trouble focusing on its goals.

One time a group of creative writers developed a habit of communicating with excessive sarcastic remarks. This was perceived by some as a way of displaying the superiority of certain highly regarded members. Their meetings were often loud, with everyone trying to assert their ideas. Once they recognized that sarcasm was rampant and potentially destructive, group members took the next step. They decided not to use sarcasm in their discussions any more. Humor was fine, but whenever sarcasm slipped out, group members comfortably reminded the offender of their mutual commitment to eliminate it. Future interactions were more positive, and the group was able to accomplish much more as a result.

Chaotic groups are typically very energetic, to the point where they are out of control. They need help harnessing all that energy. Once this is done, they focus more effectively toward accomplishing the desired objective. Here are some ways you can help:

- Point out any behavior that is destructive and remind the group members that they must respect one another and all ideas. "There seems to be a lot of sarcasm. How is this impacting you?" "I'm noticing quite a lot of interrupting. Has anyone else? What suggestions do you have for improving in this area?"

- Praise the group on its high energy level, and remind members that they need to focus by increasing the level of listening, and concentrating on the goal. "You have a tremendous amount of energy and enthusiasm. Let's work on focusing that energy by listening to everyone's ideas. We will then be able to accomplish our goal more quickly and effectively."

- Remind the group to eliminate personal attacks and step in to halt any that occur. "One thing we must not tolerate is personal attacks. If you have a concern, please offer it without insult."

Interventions

How does the facilitator assist a group in managing conflict? You help a group by making an *intervention*. An intervention is anything the facilitator does or says to alter the behavior of an individual or a group.

When should an intervention be considered? When there is any disagreement, conflict or concern whether it is stated or underlying. You do not always see a clear-cut need to make an intervention, but there are things to consider in deciding whether an intervention should be made or not.

If there is any disagreement or concern within the group, you should consider making an intervention. If the issue is a relatively minor one, such as group members arriving late, you wait to see if this happens a couple of times. There could be a legitimate reason why members are late the first time. If this is turning into a pattern, then you would probably make an intervention to point it out. Examples that might need an intervention would be:

- Regular use of sarcasm by the group.
- Constant interrupting by the group.
- Established pattern of tardiness by the group or an individual.
- A regular habit of dominating the discussion by an individual.
- Continued lack of participation by the group or an individual.

If any of these examples occurred once, you would not need to make an intervention. You should wait to see if a pattern has developed. But, don't wait too long. Avoiding an intervention when you know one is needed just prolongs the problem, making it more difficult for the group or individual to change when you finally point it out.

If you're ever in a situation where you just aren't sure whether to make an intervention, use this process. Consider the benefits and disadvantages of intervening. Ask yourself, "If I make this intervention, what could happen that would help the group or individual? What could happen that would hurt?" If the benefits outweigh the risks, then make the intervention.

This line of thinking is often pursued when investing money in the stock market, making a major purchase, or taking some other risk. First, you identify all the good things that could happen if you go ahead with the action. If you invest in that Internet company, how would you benefit? Then, you think about everything that could possibly go wrong. What's the down side of investing in that company? Could I possibly lose all my money? Ultimately, you have to decide if the potential benefits outweigh the potential risks.

You should *always* make an intervention in two instances. The first one is if the group's progress toward its desired outcome is stalled. If this occurs, try to analyze what is happening and what's preventing the group from moving forward. One example is if the group decides to vote to narrow down a list. If they can't agree on the number of votes to use, they become deadlocked on this issue for several minutes. This situation calls for an intervention. Another example is if the group needs to make a decision on whether to follow one course of action or another, and they can't reach an agreement. You could help by stepping in to make an intervention.

It isn't always easy to figure out what is preventing a group from progressing. If you notice a lot of awkward silences, you probably have a group who submerges conflict. If this delays the group's progress, you definitely need to check it out. You may have to call a break and intervene with some of the individual group members, hoping someone opens up.

There are also times when one or two individuals delay the group's progress. They are probably not aware they have this effect. Someone could be habitually not following one of the ground rules, or there may be an ongoing conflict between two group members. You would need to intervene by speaking with the individuals in private.

The second time you *always* make an intervention is when there is a personal attack. Whether the group's progress is delayed or not, a personal attack must be addressed immediately. You should point it out and explain why it is inappropriate, even if it means interrupting the speaking individual. "We've agreed that personal attacks are not acceptable behavior. Please refrain from the name-calling and stick to the issues."

Types of Situations that Need an Intervention

Once you analyze the situation and decide that an intervention is appropriate or necessary, you should identify the type of situation you are facing. There are three types of situations in which an intervention is applied. They are changing behavior, reaching consensus and gaining management support. Each type of situation requires a slightly different approach.

You intervene to change behavior when an individual member or several group members are doing something that is causing problems or preventing the group from progressing. Examples are being overly dominant during discussions, excessively criticizing the group or each other, communication style conflicts, and repeated interrupting of each other. This intervention is done in private when an individual is involved and is addressed to the group as a whole when the behavior is widespread.

The second type of situation for intervening is when a group has trouble reaching consensus. This occurs when two or more individuals can't reach an agreement on an issue and the progress of the group is halted. This could be a disagreement on process or content issues. In either case, the lack of consensus delays the group and they can't move forward without resolving their disagreement.

The third type of situation in which you would intervene is gaining management support. This is done with the group's manager in private. This type of intervention occurs when other interventions have been attempted; you and the group have tried to solve the issue and have been unsuccessful. This type of intervention should include a suggested plan of action because managers prefer being presented a problem only if there is also a solution. You know more about the issue than the manager, so it makes sense that you would also have a solution.

Figure 5.2 outlines the three types of situations that need an intervention. It also gives examples of what to look for in deciding how to intervene. There are many situations that could arise, but these three types of situations give you the most common scenarios.

Figure 5.2

Situations for Interventions

To Change Behavior	One group member:	Never follows a ground rule
		Constantly interrupts
		Consistently disagrees
		Always dominates the conversation
		Never contributes to the discussion
	Group members:	Do not follow a ground rule
		Constantly interrupt each other
		Do not contribute to the discussion
		Have trouble following commitments they've made
		Avoid disagreements on a regular basis
To Resolve Conflict	Two or more members:	Cannot reach an agreement on an issue
		Become angry or frustrated with each other
To Gain Managerial Support		Any problem situation that has not been resolved by facilitator's repeated interventions.

Intervening to Change Behavior

The more often you facilitate, the more opportunity you have to make an intervention that changes behavior. As you constantly monitor the group member's behavior, you will find opportunities to help the group work together more effectively. It is not always comfortable to address what you've observed. This process will make it easier, once you familiarize yourself with it.

When you intervene with an individual, always do so in private, so that you do not put him or her on the defensive in front of others. First, describe what you've observed to the group member. Ask the individual if he or she is aware of it. "There's something I'd like to discuss with you. I've noticed that you give a considerable amount of input, to the extent that other group members are struggling to participate in the discussion. Have you noticed this?"

Next, ask this person what he or she thinks the impact of this problem might be. "How do you think this is impacting you?" The group member may not be able to answer this question, so be ready to explain what you think the impact might be.

"Group members may not be as open to your ideas if they feel that one person is dominating the discussion. I've also noticed some restlessness when you are sharing your ideas."

Ask the individual what changes he or she could make to become a more effective group member. It is more powerful to encourage the individual to develop an improved course of action than to try to direct that person's behavior; he or she will be more committed to a personalized course of action. Ask, "How could you be more effective in the group?"

Be ready to offer your own suggestions if the person you are working with cannot think of any specific ways to improve. For example, you could say, "Limit the number of times you participate during a session and draw in participation from other group members."

I have used this method on a regular basis with individuals. One of my clients was consistently late, he did not keep his commitments, and generally made my job difficult. I used this method to point this out, hoping that he was open to hearing this feedback. He thanked me for my candidness and seemed to have even more respect for me afterwards. In time, we developed a strong working relationship.

You can also use this process to point out a widespread pattern of behavior that is slowing the group's productivity. For example, the group of creative writers widespread sarcasm that was discussed previously. I followed the same steps to address the group as a whole.

First, I discussed what I was observing and asked if anyone else noticed the same behavior. "I've noticed a lot of sarcasm in how you communicate with each other. Has anyone else noticed this?" I then gave them time to discuss their observations. After they discussed their perceptions of the issue, I asked, "How do you think this impacts the group as a whole?"

I made sure that I was ready to point out the impact myself in case group members could not think of anything. In this case, they quickly realized how destructive their use of sarcasm was. Some members didn't realize they were offending others and were feeling contrite. I asked them how they could be more effective as a team, or what they could do to eliminate this behavior pattern. They concluded that they should stop using sarcasm, add this commitment to their ground rules, and remind each other if someone forgets.

Intervening to Help Two or More Individuals Reach a Consensus

There are times when group members struggle to reach an agreement at a decision point. You can be very valuable in helping them consider the different views and then find an avenue that everyone can support. The following process is a method that can be used to help two or more individuals resolve conflict. Resolving conflict means reaching an agreement on how the parties involved either prevent the conflict from recurring or develop a plan of action to deal with this conflict that is acceptable to all members.

Here are the steps to follow. First, get group members to discuss the issue openly and honestly by asking for people to share their views. You could say, "It seems that you are not seeing eye to eye on this issue. Let's discuss why each of you feels the way you do." This will help the group clear up any misunderstandings and clarify both areas of agreement and disagreement. They may need your help in pointing out the specific areas in which they agree and the specific areas in which they disagree. An example would be, "It seems that everyone agrees on the date of the product rollout; but many of you are not in agreement on how much to spend on advertising. Am I correct?"

Getting people to express and analyze each others' views is important. If members at least feel they are heard and understood, they are more likely to support a decision that was not necessarily their first choice. It may also help to get people to understand the "why" behind each opinion being expressed. This may help the group consider something important that hasn't been mentioned yet.

Once the problem or issue has been thoroughly discussed, get the group to generate possible ideas for resolving the issue. To accomplish this, you can ask one or more of the following questions, depending on the specific issue:

What should you do to make sure this doesn't happen again?

What would have to happen in order for all of you to support this?

What ideas do you have to prevent this in the future?

Once the group discusses a sufficient number of options for resolving the issue, lead the group to a resolution. The group will hopefully reach a consensus on how they'll solve the problem or address the issue.

Here's a simple example of how the intervention process works. Suppose a group wants a chocolate bar that will be divided up for each group member. But, they don't agree on what kind of chocolate to purchase. Subgroup A wants a plain chocolate bar and subgroup B wants one with peanuts. As all issues are discussed and clarified, the group makes a discovery. Subgroup A members don't want a peanut chocolate bar because they hate peanuts. However, subgroup B doesn't necessarily have to have a bar with peanuts; any type of nut will do. So the group decides on an almond chocolate bar. While this is a very simple example, it is not unlike many situations in which groups can't reach a consensus. The facilitator can help a group explore the areas of disagreement fully enough to also realize the areas of agreement. This makes reaching consensus more possible.

For example, imagine a session in which a group of mid-level managers represent two functions in the organization, marketing and engineering. The marketing people are selling services that the engineering department does not deliver on time. This conflict concerning delivery dates has to be resolved in order to meet customer requirements. A good facilitator can help by generating discussion around marketing's preferred time frames for the specific products. The group would be asked to generate possible ideas to help engineering meet the time frames, or ideas for how marketing could revise the dates without alienating any customers. After formulating a plan that addresses current delivery times that are behind schedule, they might reach a better agreement that improves future effective communication. Marketing is given specific time frames for specific products (with some negotiating so that they could keep up with competition), and engineering is promised more advance notice on future client requirements. This is only a fictitious example, but it shows how a consensus is reached with a facilitator generating a discussion around the issues.

Intervening to Gain Managerial Support

The intervention designed to get management support is used as a last resort. You need it when you have already intervened to change behavior several times on a specific issue, the behavior remains unchanged, and the group's progress is seriously delayed. Another instance you would need management support is when you have repeatedly intervened to help the group reach a consensus on a specific decision point and group members are still struggling, thus impacting their ability to reach an agreement that everyone supports. So, an intervention with the group's manager is used when you, the facilitator have intervened several times with no success. Here are some examples:

- A difficult group member prevents the group from progressing because of his/her behavior. You already spoke privately with him on several occasions. He did not make any changes for the better.
- Difficulties have arisen with group members tendency to interrupt each other. You initiated discussions about this several times. The group just can't seem to make improvements and this has greatly reduced their productivity.
- There is an unclear understanding of management expectations of what the group should accomplish. The group has become paralyzed and is not progressing. You clarified their areas of confusion but realize that only their manager can answer their questions.
- The group needs an unanticipated resource. They need approval from their manager because they don't have the authority to get this resource themselves.

Since managers generally like problems and solutions presented together, here is the best way to gain managerial support. First, point out the positive aspects of what the group is working on. "We are working within the budget that you've set for us, and are considering some cost saving measures." This begins your discussion on a positive note. You want the manager to know the group is accomplishing something valuable.

Next, discuss the problem or need clearly and concisely. "We are having a problem with one group member. John Smith's dominating behavior, while we've discussed this with him at length, is continuing to be a problem." Explain the problem and also describe what was attempted to resolve the problem.

Then, make your recommendation or suggest a solution and clearly state the anticipated benefit. "I think he should be removed from the group and sent back to his previous job position. This way, the group will be able to finish the project on time." The manager may want some additional information from you. Answer his questions concisely. Lastly, ask for the manager's approval. "Can I get your approval on this?"

I worked with a group consisting of a variety of job positions including both front line people and corporate people. One of the corporate people, we'll call him "Joe," was designated as the group's subject-matter expert because of his vast experience. However, Joe was not considered competent in that particular area so the group needed information. This came up in several discussions when the group needed more expertise from the area he represented. After facilitating a very candid discussion in which the group expressed their concerns without offending Joe, everyone decided (including Joe) that he was not a good match for the group's needs. I went to the manager and recommended that Joe be placed in a different role for the project — one which blended better with his knowledge. I also recommended placing a new member in the group so that the original need for a subject-matter expert was filled. Everyone ended up very satisfied with this change, including Joe. He certainly was not incompetent; he was simply in the wrong role.

Chapter Summary

There Are No Magic Formulas

This chapter has outlined the major types of conflict and the ways in which groups typically address such disagreements. It is important to get group members to verbalize their disagreements so they can have the opportunity to resolve. Conflict is healthy, as long as it is addressed and resolved.

What Is Conflict?

Conflict is a disagreement within the group that is significant enough to slow down or halt the group's progress. Process, content, and communication style conflict are the three types that groups display, with content conflict the most desirable because it focuses groups on the most important issues that bring about the best solutions.

How Groups Respond to Conflict

Groups typically approach conflict by avoiding it (submerged), addressing it (healthy) or excessively arguing about it (chaotic). Groups that submerge conflict are challenging because they often don't open up. Chaotic groups are very open, but have trouble reaching a resolution for the conflict that emerges. The facilitator strives to guide the group into the healthy range, where conflict is addressed and resolved.

Interventions

An intervention is anything a facilitator says or does to alter the behavior of an individual or a group. Sometimes the decision to intervene is a judgment call, when the problem is relatively minor. An intervention is usually not needed unless a specific behavior or problem becomes a pattern.

Making an intervention becomes an obligation when the groups' progress is delayed or stalled, or a personal attack was made by one group member toward another.

Types of Situations that Need an Intervention

There are three types of situations in which an intervention is possible. The first is to change an established behavior pattern by an individual or a group. The second is to help two or more individuals reach a consensus when they have had difficulty doing so. The third is used as a last resort. When the first two interventions have failed to produce any improvement, an intervention to gain managerial support.

There is no group whose members will be able to agree on each and every issue presented. In order to reach a specified goal, sometimes a group must "agree to disagree" and find the solution that has the best chance of gaining support. Your role is to encourage group members to resolve the disagreements as best as they can. There is no proven formula that will make this happen every time there is conflict. You will learn much from experience — by making mistakes and achieving successes. Since you are dealing with human beings, the conflicts that arise are different every time. The more difficult the situations you facilitate, the more proficient you'll become at handling them.

CHAPTER

6

How Can We Get Things Done?

Dan, the project manager: "All I ever seem to do is put out fires! I keep fixing the same problems over and over again. I can't seem to find time for eliminating the problems. I simply put bandages over them. They inevitably come back to haunt me."

As human beings, we face challenges every day, just like this project manager. Yet, some people overcome obstacles better than others. What gives some of us the ability to set a goal, decide what it takes to reach that goal, and then achieve it? Luck is sometimes a factor, but an unreliable one. Is it talent? Talent does help, but there are many talented people who never seem to get anything accomplished.

So, what does it take? A well-thought-out, structured plan is the best method for accomplishing worthy goals for both individuals and groups. Groups and individuals, like Dan, need a bit of structure in order to exercise creativity and talent for the purpose of setting goals that improve the organization. These structures are called process models. They contain prescribed steps that illustrate the steps necessary to accomplish a goal. They eliminate frustration because they help groups and individuals deal with issues systematically. This chapter will describe one process model that groups can use to organize their work. It is called PROBE.

You will learn how to guide groups through the different phases of PROBE. This model helps you organize the group's approach, depending on the type of goal the group wants to accomplish. If there is something in the organization that is not working properly, such as equipment breaking down, people not performing their jobs quickly enough, or errors made, you would guide the group through the PROBE process model to solve a problem. If there is simply a decision to be made, or an opportunity to take advantage of within the organization, (such as a new product), designing a new procedure or planning an event, then you would guide the group through the PROBE model. PROBE can be used for either of these situations, solving problems or addressing opportunities.

Overview of PROBE

Each letter of the PROBE process model represents a specific function. Figure 6.1 outlines what each letter stands for. P stands for Projection. The first thing that must be done to solve a problem or address an opportunity is to describe the situation and project what action will be taken. This is usually done with a measurement such as reducing errors by 50 percent or increasing product sales by 20 percent.

The next step, R, stands for root cause analysis, which means finding the real cause of the problem. During this phase, if the group is solving a problem, members must collect information to identify factors that are causing the problem. This encourages elimination or reduction. If the group is addressing an opportunity, there is no need for root cause analysis, so the group skips over this phase and moves on to the next one.

The next phase is O, or options phase. This is where the group discusses options for eliminating root causes if they are solving a problem. If the group is addressing an opportunity, they identify options for doing so. Once those options are identified, the group evaluates and chooses the best options, which is the B phase in the process model.

After group members evaluate and select best options, they develop a plan for implementing them. This is the last phase, E for execute.

The different phases in the PROBE model can be used in a number of ways, depending upon how much authority the group is given or what

Figure 6.1

The Probe Process Model

Process Model	Phases Defined
PROBE	P = Projection
	R = Root cause
	O = Options
	B = Best option
	E = Execute

they were asked to accomplish. For example, imagine that the group is being asked by senior management to only identify what is causing unusually low productivity by service technicians. They would only need to use the first two phases of the PROBE model. As their facilitator, you should help them develop a projection to define the problem and project exactly how much they can increase productivity. It might be helpful to know current productivity levels and compare this to the expected levels. This is the first phase, P. Next, you guide them through the R phase to find the root cause of the problem. At this point they would have fulfilled the management directive.

Another example is if the root cause of the low productivity is already identified. Imagine that a new piece of equipment used by service technicians was doubling their installation time, because they were using it incorrectly. The group is being asked to eliminate the main cause (new equipment being used incorrectly) that is contributing to the problem (low productivity during installations). Since they know the cause, they now have to identify options for eliminating it. This is what takes place in the O and B phases. You facilitate group members as they identify possible options for eliminating the cause such as training service technicians on the new equipment, coaching them on the job, or even sending the new equipment back to the supplier and using the old equipment again. This is the O phase. In the B phase, group members decide which of those options are the best ones to implement.

What if a sales group was asked to penetrate a new market? They could use the O, B, and E, phases to identify possible markets for penetration, choose the best markets and develop a plan for making it happen.

A final example for using PROBE would be if the decision were already made and the group is simply asked to design a plan for carrying it out. Imagine that your group is asked to have a conference to kick off the unveiling of a new product. This is the E phase, or Execution. You would guide the group toward developing a plan of action for this event.

Of course, the group could be charged with carrying out the entire project from start to finish, in which case they would follow the entire PROBE model. Whether the group is using the entire PROBE process, or pieces of it, anticipate that they will need a considerable amount of time. It could take anywhere from one meeting to 20 meetings or more, depending upon how much of PROBE is utilized and what the specific situation is. Work needs to be done both inside and outside of the meetings. For example, if gathering information to find the root cause (R phase), group members would probably decide on what information merits gathering during a meeting. They would most likely make arrangements to gather it outside of meetings.

You can also use PROBE as an individual. I use this process model all the time. After I wrote the manuscript for this book, I realized I needed to find a publisher. I followed the O, B, and E steps to help me do this. First, I identified a list of approximately 200 publishers; this is the O phase. Next, I chose 60 publishers I thought would find my manuscript interesting based on the types of books they published. This was the B phase. In the E phase, I listed all the actions needed to get these 60 publishers interested in my work. I put together a package that included a book outline, a cover letter, and the first three chapters of my manuscript. This package was sent out to all 60 publishers. This resulted in finding an excellent publisher, Oasis Press.

How to Use PROBE

You need to fully understand how to use PROBE so that you can successfully lead the group in solving problems. You will also want to educate your group on how it works, so they understand the logic behind it. Understanding when to use the different phases will be helpful in determining where to start. This is the first step in guiding the group toward the successful accomplishment of the desired goal.

Figure 6.2

PROBE Model Process Tools

1. Develop **P**rojection:	Goal statement
2. Find **R**oot Cause:	Check sheet, flow chart, or survey
3. List **O**ptions:	Brainstorm or round robin
	Clarify
	Combine
	Categorize
4. Pick **B**est Option:	Eliminate the obvious
	Multi-vote
	Compare against criteria
5. **E**xecute:	Action plan time line

The next step is selecting the appropriate process tools. As discussed previously, a process tool is a structured method the group follows when identifying causes of problems, creating options, and designing plans for implementing decisions. A common process tool, brainstorming, is mentioned in this book several times. Figure 6.2 illustrates a repertoire of process tools in each phase of PROBE. This section describes how each of the process tools are used and under what circumstances you should recommend them to the group.

Develop a Projection

This first phase, Develop a Projection, helps group members anticipate what action will be taken (in measurable terms). They also need to include any limits they must work within, as well as describing how the organization would benefit. This is called a goal statement.

Here's an example. I worked with a cable company that was having problems with excessive outages. (Outages occur when an entire geographic area loses the connection going into customer homes.) Company management formed a group to include employees in various job positions who had different perspectives on the problem, including service technicians, customer service reps, a dispatcher, a customer service supervisor, and a service tech supervisor. The group's task was to reach an agreement on what action would be taken, how much of the problem could realistically be solved, what the parameters are and how the company would benefit from their efforts. With some input from the operations manager, they agreed that they should be able to reduce outages by 25 percent. The operations manager also restricted them to some parameters. Group members would have to continue their current responsibilities while working to solve this problem. They could not hire or re-assign additional employees to cover themselves. As their facilitator, I helped them write a goal statement. First, I coached them on how to develop one and then facilitated a discussion in which they decided what the statement would say. Here's what they came up with.

> We will reduce outages by 25 percent in a way that maintains current headcount so that our customers will be more satisfied with our service.

How do you help a group write a goal statement like the one that was developed by the cable company? First, explain to the group that three elements need to be included in it. First, the group must identify a measurable action that will be taken. There should also be an explanation of any parameters that the group must maintain, such as budget, time, productivity, policies, regulations, or headcount. The third element necessary is a description of how the organization will benefit.

It often helps to suggest a structure for the goal statement.

- We will ... (Describe the measurable action to be taken.)
- In a way that ... (Describe any parameters that must be maintained)
- So that ... (Describe how the organization will benefit.)

Examples of a Goal Statement

Here are examples of fictitious situations. Listed next to each situation is a correctly written goal statement.

> A group from a power company is trying to reduce the number of power outages that occur each quarter by 10 percent. It is working with a tight budget. This is a problem.

Goal statement: *We will* reduce quarterly outages by 10 percent *in a way that* maintains our current budget *so that* we can improve customer satisfaction.

A group from a lumber company is trying to reduce the amount of time it takes to process an order from three to two weeks. There were complaints from customers that it takes too long to receive products. This is a problem.

Goal statement: *We will* reduce the product order process by one week *in a way* that maintains current headcount *so that* we can get orders to our customers faster and maintain our current customer base while adding new customers.

A hospital emergency unit has low employee morale. There have been an unusually high number of anonymous employee complaints sent to human resources. Group members want to reduce the number of complaints by 50 percent. Work on this project must be done during non-peak hours. This is a problem.

Goal statement: We will reduce employee complaints by 50 percent in a way that work being done on this occurs during non-peak hours so that we can improve employee morale.

A group from a software company is asked to create some new applications for a popular software product. They must create these applications for use by current markets, not any new markets. This will help them create more revenue within current markets. This is an opportunity.

Goal statement: We will identify five new applications for the LINK system in a way that current markets will be able to use them so that the company will have additional revenue streams with current customers.

---

goal statement is typically developed in one meeting. For example, in the case of the power company trying to reduce power outages by ten percent, the goal statement would be developed in the first meeting. The intended meeting outcome might be: A goal statement to address the outage problem. While it takes one meeting to actually develop a goal statement, it takes several meetings to accomplish the specified goal.

This is the difference between an intended meeting outcome and a goal statement. A goal statement defines and sets measurable actions concerning the overall situation. The steps toward achieving these actions, (the PROBE model), will be followed in several meetings over a period of time. The intended outcome statements in each of these meetings will point out which step in PROBE that is currently followed as the group makes its way toward solving the problem.

Achieving the intended meeting outcome versus accomplishing the overall goal is much like winning the battle versus winning the war. If you win enough battles, you'll probably win the war. If you achieve enough meeting outcome statements, you'll most likely accomplish the overall goal. Meeting outcome statements are like the small battles you fight in order to reach the overall goal — winning the war.

Target the Root Cause of the Problem

When you target root cause, you are trying to find out what is causing a problem. This is something people do in a variety of situations as individuals and as groups. I like to snow ski, and I'm just good enough to be dangerous. Sometimes, I pick up speed more quickly than I can handle. When I make my turns, I know I'm supposed to dig into the snow with the edges of my skis, but it doesn't always happen. If I'm having a particularly difficult time doing this, which would mean I'm making a lot of "face plants" in the snow, I do a quick "root cause analysis" to assess what's causing this. First, I check out my boots because if they're not snug enough, it's more difficult to turn. Then, I try to notice if I'm leaning into the fronts of my skis enough. This helps with balance. Lastly, I evaluate whether I'm digging the edges of my skis into the snow. This gives me control. Usually it's the edges that are a problem. Once I identify what's causing my uncontrollable speed, I can correct the problem. Skiing on my feet is much more fun than skiing on any other body part.

To do a good job of root cause analysis in a business situation, information about the problem must be gathered and discussed, much like the discussion that takes place concerning a problem with poor skiing. The group needs to determine the *origin* of the problem, which is defined as the factor or factors making the biggest contribution to the problem. These are considered the root causes of the problem. They must be found and eliminated in order to solve the problem.

Remember, if your group is not dealing with a problem, then searching for a cause is not necessary. Addressing an opportunity does not require an identification of what is causing the problem, because there is nothing really going wrong. So, you would guide the group past this phase and into the next one — O for Options.

There are many different ways to gather information about a problem. We will focus on three process tools used for this purpose: the check sheet, the flow chart, and the survey.

A check sheet is a tool used to keep track of the number of times potential causes of a problem are occurring. Examples of causes that might be monitored are time units, types of defects, or events. Since there is rarely only one cause that is creating a problem, the check sheet identifies how often several potential causes are occurring so that those causes occurring the most stand out.

When using the check sheet, it's important to both gather data and organize the different types of data so that analyzing is easier. To help a group develop a check sheet, ask them to identify possible causes that contribute to the problem. As each potential cause surfaces, write it down on the flip chart. Once the group has reviewed the list of causes and agrees that these are the right causes to investigate, you should then get group members to determine the period of time in which the causes will be tracked; one week, one month, or some other period of time. The developed check sheet is then given to those on the job who have the most exposure to what needs to be monitored. Another option would be to get volunteers within the group to go through the records to investigate incidences of the listed causes.

For example, if the power company employees who wanted to reduce outages by 10 percent developed a check sheet. This could be done during a meeting in which the intended outcome is a check sheet for reducing outages.

Group members could brainstorm a list of potential causes for outages. This list could be given to three group members who begin tracking any outages that occurred during the previous quarter. Wherever the records showed that one occurred, they could research work orders to find out what caused that particular outage. These occurrences would be documented as shown in Figure 6.3. The group could get back together within two weeks to examine a summary report of these causes. Figure 6.3 shows the final numbers that might be presented to the group. This list is only an

Figure 6.3

Example of a Check Sheet

Causes of Outages Third Quarter	Number of Occurrences
Inclement weather	10
Technician's error	15
Traffic accident	8
Equipment breakdown	30
Other	7

example and would in actuality be much longer. Also, after examining the results of the first collection of data, the group might decide to do some additional data gathering. For example, they may decide to find out which equipment is failing and causing outages since the number of occurrences is 30. Or, they may decide to find out which technicians' errors had caused outages, since the check sheet indicates there might be a problem with an unnamed technician. It's like peeling back the layers of an onion. You sometimes need several phases of data collection to find the real cause of a problem.

The second process tool that could be used in determining root cause is called the flow chart. A flow chart depicts a concept in the format of a picture or diagram and is a particularly useful tool for illustrating procedures or multi-step processes. It presents information about a problem involving work procedures, such as a service order process, a billing process, contract administration, the hiring procedure, a payroll process and even employee disciplinary process.

If you determine that your group's problem involves how well or how quickly things are carried out in a specific work procedure, then you should recommend that the group develop a flow chart. Guide the group toward identifying all the actual steps in the process that require examination, in order of occurrence. Write these steps on the flip chart, as each group member calls it out. Emphasize that they will first identify how things are actually being done currently, not how they think things should be done. Next, have the group identify the type of function that is taking place within each step; decisions, control/inspection, operation, movement or delay.

For example, consider the case of the lumber company trying to reduce the amount of time it takes to process orders from three weeks to two weeks. Group members would most likely decide to analyze what currently occurs in the ordering process to determine if they could speed things up without increasing errors in the orders. They would need to chart the steps the current ordering process follows. Once this is done, the group would determine where improvements could be made. Figure 6.4 shows a flow chart that signifies an ordering process. A flow chart should designate who is doing what, the department in which the activity takes place, and the amount of time for each activity. The ordering process illustrated here indicates it takes approximately 15 business days (three weeks) from the day the order is received to the day the order is shipped. Figure 6.5 signifies the meaning of the symbols used in the flow chart. These symbols indicate the type of function that is taking place in each step.

Once the group sees the whole picture, it is easier to analyze. To analyze and improve a process, the facilitator asks the group to look for the following possibilities:

- Are there any steps that are unnecessary and need elimination?
- Are there any steps that could be combined into one step?
- Are there any delays that occur between steps? Often, the problems lie between the steps, not within them. The group should be encouraged to examine this.
- Are there steps that occur in the same department within different areas of the process? For example, if the process begins in accounting, then goes to the warehouse and then back to accounting it could be possible to keep the process in accounting for all the steps, and then send it to the warehouse. This saves time.
- What would the ideal process look like? Sometimes it helps to throw out the current process and start over.

After group members determine ways to improve the process, they can start to incorporate these changes into the work environment. This should be done while monitoring the effect closely.

Figure 6.4

Example of a Flow Chart

The following flow chart shows how an order is processed.

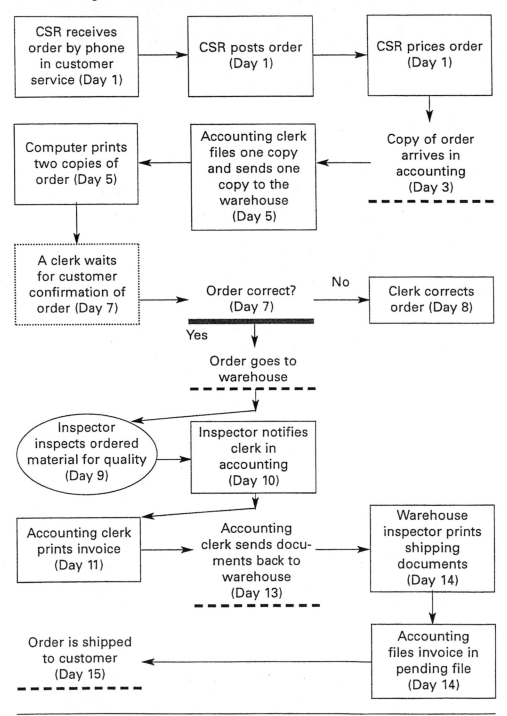

Figure 6.5

Flow Chart Symbols

Decisions	▬▬▬▬▬
Control/inspection	(ellipse)
Operation	(rectangle)
Movement	▬ ▬ ▬ ▬ ▬ ▬
Delay	(dotted rectangle)

The third process tool that helps a group find the root cause is the survey. A survey is a list of questions asking people for their opinions of an issue. You would use a survey when there is a low opinion about some issue and you want to find out what is causing this low opinion. For example, it is common practice for organizations to find out how they can improve the level of customer service by using surveys that ask customers questions about their experiences when doing business with the company. Written surveys can be administered to an entire population or a sample population. Surveys can also be administered verbally by phone, in focus groups or one-on-one.

If you are working with a group that needs to ask for opinions and perceptions of a specific audience, the first step is to ask the group to brainstorm different questions to ask the audience to get the necessary information. Write these down and get agreement from the group on both wording and content. After group members have developed their list of questions, ask them who should be surveyed — the entire population or just a sampling? They also need to decide how the survey will be administered — in writing, in person, in focus groups, over the phone, or some other choice. The group should then decide who will administer the survey, when it will take place and who will report the results to the group. Once

Figure 6.6

Employee Survey Questions

Please answer the questions below according to the following scale: 5 is very favorable, 4 is favorable, 3 is average, 2 is low and 1 is very low.

1. How do you rate your company as a place to work?

2. How satisfied are you with your job?

3. How would you judge the ability of your manager?

4. To what extent do you feel you are kept informed of company events?

these decisions are made and the survey is administered, the group will have information on the perceptions of a problem or issue.

Consider the case of the hospital emergency unit that experiences low employee morale. If group members were to develop a survey, it might look something like Figure 6.6. However, these questions are just a sampling. In actuality, there are probably several other questions that need to be asked to get a true picture of the situation. This survey would be administered to all unit employees.

Whether you and your group use a check sheet, a flow chart, a survey, or some combination of these process tools, once you identify the root cause or causes, you are ready to move to the next phase of PROBE to identify options that eliminate these root causes.

List the Options

The O phase helps groups identify options by eliminating the root causes identified in the previous phase, or addressing opportunities that were identified in the projection phase. The options phase contains five process tools:

1. Brainstorm or Round Robin to identify the possible options.
2. Clarify any options that group members don't understand.

. Combine any similar options and incorporate into one option.
. Categorize if the group needs to organize options into main headings.

en groups like to evaluate during this phase, which is not a good idea
ou want them to fully consider all options available. Remind them that
luation will take place in the next phase — Best Options. At this point,
ourage the group to simply create a list of options and then organize
se ideas.

first step in the Options phase is to help group members create a list
ptions to eliminate root causes or address an opportunity. There are
process tools that can be used to do this, brainstorming and round
in.

instorming is defined as a spontaneous generation of ideas from all
up members. Members say the first thing that comes to their minds,
you write down their ideas on the flip chart. Brainstorming is a
thod that helps group members think of creative ideas with very little
cture.

ou have a quiet group, try the round robin process tool instead of
instorming. It gives the group more structure by allowing each group
mber to give his or her idea in turn. Just keep going from one group
mber to the next, one after the other, writing the ideas on the flip chart.
is Joseph's turn and he doesn't have any ideas, then he can pass and
try the next person. If Benny has an idea, but it isn't his turn yet,
ourage him to write it down, so he remembers it. This method makes
asier for the more silent members to give their ideas and it equalizes
up participation. Round robin does not have the same energy level
t brainstorming does, but it still encourages the group to give all their
as, even if they seem like bad ideas. Often a bad idea given by one per-
. will trigger a good idea by another person. Contributing ideas freely
ances creativity.

ending upon the issue at hand, creativity is very important. Easy
wers are not always apparent when you try to think of new ideas.
ng creative is often a challenging proposition for adults. Yet, young
dren are naturally creative. If you have spent any time around chil-
n, you know what I mean. I love watching my niece, Natalie, when she
ainting a picture, or using clay to create a sculpture. Children are nat-
lly inquisitive and open to new ideas. Unfortunately, formal education
n programs children to "spit out" the right answers so they'll receive
sing grades. As adults, this tendency to give the "right answer" can

become dominant. We assume, out of habit, that there is only one right answer to any question that must be decided.

This practice decreases creativity and limits you to a narrow field of options. In reality, there are no clear-cut answers. The welfare of your organization is dependent upon your ability to consider many options so that you can make the best decisions possible. The brainstorming and round robin process tools, when used appropriately, help you accomplish this.

Here's an example of how to help a group build a list of options. The group is having a problem with wet floors in the refrigeration area. These floors are causing accidents; employees are slipping and falling down. The group knows that the cause is the wet floors. Now they must identify some options for addressing this situation.

If you were the group's facilitator, you start by asking group members to brainstorm a list of options for eliminating the wet floors in the refrigeration area. As they "throw out" the ideas, you write them down on the flip chart. Figure 6.7 illustrates what the initial list might look like.

Figure 6.7

Possible Options to Eliminate the Wet Floors

1. Maintain refrigeration more frequently

2. Do frequent floor mopping

3. Buy newer refrigerators

4. Do frequent equipment mopping

5. Place equipment in a low or no traffic area

6. Put up signs to warn employees

7. Put a fence around the area

8. Wear flippers

9. Put down absorbent rugs

10. Don't worry about it

There are a couple of crazy ideas on this list, but this is a good sign. It means that group members are expressing their ideas freely and openly. Evaluating the ideas doesn't happen until the next step. You may have to remind group members of this if they start to say things like, "That won't work." Also, it's a good idea to number the items when writing down group member's ideas. It makes it easier as the group begins asking you to make changes to the list. Members can reference the ideas by number, so you can quickly find the referred item.

Once the group runs out of ideas, it's time to guide them toward clarifying: which is making sure all group members understand the ideas that are contributed. This is done whenever a list is generated by the group. Ask, "Which of these items do you need clarification on?" Give the group several seconds to look over the list. If a group member asks for clarification of a particular item, refer to the person who gave the idea by saying, "Who gave this idea? Jerry, could you please explain to Frank what you meant by this?" As Jerry clarifies the idea, you should write down a brief explanation next to the item being discussed.

For example, consider the independent supermarket that had the wet floors in the refrigeration area. One group member may ask for clarification of idea number 4, "doing frequent equipment mopping." If this were the case, you would need to find out who contributed this idea and then ask this person to explain the meaning of it to the group. You do not have to clarify every idea on the list, only those that the group members don't understand.

Groups will still tend to evaluate ideas during clarification. Remind them that they don't have to worry about whether they agree or disagree with any of these ideas until they get to the next phase: Pick Best Option. The clarifying tool is designed to simply help them understand each idea that's been suggested.

After clarifying ideas, it is necessary to combine them. This would happen if there were any two ideas that were really saying the same thing. To find out if there are any ideas that need combining, ask the group, "Are there any similar ideas on this list that we could combine as one item?" If there is a suggestion to combine, check with the contributors of the specific ideas before combining them. Consider the supermarket company's list of options for eliminating wet floors. The group might decide to combine numbers 2 and 4, which both relate to mopping. Then, you would cross out either number 2 or number 4 and leave the other one that was not crossed out.

It is occasionally necessary for a group to categorize a list by sorting ideas into main headings. This is used when the group wants to ensure the options being contributed represent specific main headings or themes. First, ask the group to suggest possible categories where the ideas might fit. Then, ask the group to sort the ideas into the suggested categories. Additional ideas or categories may also be generated and added to the list.

For example, the supermarket would categorize the options for eliminating wet floors if group members wanted different employees to have responsibility for the same types of duties. Figure 6.8 shows the different categories assigned to appropriate options. This makes it easier to assign duties, since each employee would be assigned a different category. One person would be in charge of the equipment, someone would handle the mopping, and a third person would be responsible for putting up the obstacles. The last idea was given a miscellaneous category because it didn't fit into any of the other categories. It will probably end up being eliminated from the list in the next phase, anyway.

Figure 6.8

Options with Their Categories

1. Maintain refrigeration more frequently — Equipment
2. Do frequent floor mopping — Mopping
3. Buy newer refrigerators — Equipment
4. Do frequent equipment mopping — Mopping
5. Place equipment in a low or no traffic area — Equipment
6. Put up signs to warn employees — Obstacles
7. Put a fence around the area — Obstacles
8. Wear flippers — Obstacles
9. Put down absorbent rugs — Obstacles
10. Don't worry about it — Miscellaneous

Once the group creates an organized list of options, they are ready to evaluate those options and pick the best ones, which is the next phase.

Choose the Best Option

There are three process tools that help a group narrow down a list of options. They are eliminate the obvious, multi-vote and compare against criteria. These three tools provide a structure in which the group evaluates the options that were created and organized in the previous phase.

To eliminate the obvious, you take a poll to find out which options group members can agree to remove from the list. This is a tool I use frequently. It's easy to use and helps in removing those items that are obviously not viable. I simply ask the group, "Which items on this list can we all quickly agree to remove because they won't work?"

Look at Figure 6.7. Imagine that after asking your group which items can be eliminated, Leo suggests that, "wearing flippers" can be eliminated. You should then check with the group to make sure there is agreement. "Is everyone in agreement that we can eliminate wearing flippers?" If everyone agrees, draw a line through the item in question. Then ask the group if anything else can be eliminated. If Lana suggests eliminating another item, "putting down absorbent rugs," you would again check with the rest of the group. If anyone has reservations about this new suggestion to eliminate an item, you would say, "Let's leave it up there for now."

Eliminate the obvious is used to eliminate only those items that clearly won't work. If there is a reservation from any one member, the item should be left on the list for future consideration.

The next process tool to use is multi-vote. It is a method used to help a group narrow a list and determine the most important options through the use of voting. Multi-vote can also be used to prioritize a list from most important to least important.

To use multi-vote to narrow a list, you should recommend the number of votes each group member will have. This can be a random number or a good rule of thumb is to divide the number of items on the list by three. You can also ask group members to weigh their votes by allowing them to assign up to a certain number of votes on any one option. Give the group a few minutes to decide where they will cast their votes. They may want to jot this down on scrap paper. Tabulate the votes by calling out each item on the list and asking members who voted for that item to raise their hands. Write down the total number of votes for each item next to the item that is listed on the flip chart. Avoid tabulating votes by asking each group member one at a time, as this would give the last few group members an opportunity to change their votes, based on which items have the most votes. After completing the tabulation of votes, those ideas with the most votes provide a picture of the group's interest.

Figure 6.9 gives you an example of the supermarket list with the tabulation of votes. After reviewing this list, you will see that the group clearly wants to handle the problem by focusing on the refrigeration equipment and mopping because those items concerning refrigeration received the most votes.

Multi-voting is also used to prioritize a list, ranking items from most important to least important, or vice versa. To do this, follow the process for voting to narrow a list. Once the votes have been tabulated, remind group members they will keep everything on the list, but they have to rank order them. The item with the most number of votes would be put at the top of the list. The item with the second most number of votes would be

Figure 6.9

List of Options

1. Maintain refrigeration more frequently — 15
2. Do frequent floor mopping — 10
3. Buy newer refrigerators — 5
4. Do frequent equipment mopping — 12
5. Place equipment in a low or no traffic area — 4
6. Put up signs to warn employees — 4
7. Put a fence around the area — 1
8. Wear flippers — 0
9. Put down absorbent rugs — 0
10. Don't worry about it — 0

Figure 6.10

List of Options Prioritized

1. Maintain refrigeration frequently (15)

2. Place equipment in a low or no traffic area (14)

3. Do frequent equipment mopping (12)

4. Do frequent mopping (10)

5. Buy newer refrigerators (5)

6. Put up signs to warn employees (4)

7. Put a fence around the area

put next, and so on. If there are tied items, the group would decide which one goes in front of the other. Figure 6.10 shows the supermarket's list of options in a prioritized format.

Prioritizing is useful in helping groups sort out what's most important when there is a limited budget or limited time. Both multi-vote and prioritize are valuable tools for showing a clear picture on where the group stands as a whole.

Another tool that can be used to choose the best option is compare against criteria. This process tool helps the group identify criteria against which to compare their options. It works best when the group has used eliminate the obvious and multi-vote to narrow the list first. Then, when there are three to eight items left, compare against criteria can be used.

Here's how to use compare against criteria. First, ask group members to identify some criteria that they think is important in choosing the best options. Write down their ideas on the flip chart. Then introduce a scale from zero to three, which measures the extent that each of the options meets each of the criteria. This gives a picture of how each option measures up against the criteria. Figure 6.11 gives an example of this tool with a group of hiring managers choosing the best candidates for three account executive positions that need to be filled. After looking at the "Total" column, it's clear that the three top candidates are Carol, Vincent, and Lisa.

Figure 6.11

Compare Against Criteria

	Years in Sales	High Energy	Self-Motivated	MBA	Total
Gina	2	2	2	2	8
Dave	3	1	2	0	6
Lisa	2	3	3	3	11
Carol	3	3	3	3	12
Vincent	3	3	3	3	12

Code

0 = does not meet criteria

1 = partially meets criteria

2 = meets criteria

3 = exceeds

Compare against criteria gives groups a way of objectively choosing the best options, and it also ensures that there is some discussion around the value of the options being considered. Even if the group does not use compare against criteria, members should thoroughly discuss the pros and cons of each of the options, until they reach a consensus. We have discussed how to help a group reach a consensus in Chapters 4 and 5. Here is a review of some of them:

- Ask for everyone's input, so the group can consider both sides of the issue.
- When there is a disagreement, ask those with opposing opinions to explain why they have a particular opinion.
- Discourage the group from voting when there are only two or three options left and the group must choose one option. Encourage discussion instead.

If is often difficult for a group to make a decision, yet members are responsible for their own success. You cannot make the decision for them. You can only strive to help them consider all the issues, and support them in whatever decision is made.

Execute the Best Option

One question I am constantly asked is how I had the courage to start my own consulting business. Personally, it was more a matter of fear than courage. Eleven years ago, I was single, lived in a small apartment, and I was out of a job. Although this was a scary scenario, how I got into this situation is of no consequence now; how I got myself out of it is relevant to this discussion. I had always had a dream of starting my own consulting business. I figured that it was time to give it my best shot. So, I set up an "office" on my dining room table, made some phone calls, and started asking lots of questions to consulting acquaintances. From these discussions, I developed a plan of action. I identified everything I needed to do to get my business started. Then I started to take action by following my plan. I knew I wasn't the most talented, the most well-known, or the most aggressive consultant. But where there's a will and an action plan, there's a way! Over the last 11 years, I've had a lot of rewards and more fun than I ever imagined.

Action planning is what occurs in the Execute phase, once group members have decided on the best options from the previous phase. Now it's time for them to make things happen by implementing their decisions, as I did with my consulting practice. There is basically one process tool for this phase, the action plan time line.

An action plan is a logical sequence of activities for implementing a group's decision and following through on that decision. An action plan is a schedule that outlines the tasks that need to be done, who is responsible for doing them, and when each of these tasks will be completed. The timing of the activities can be depicted in a graph or time line.

To help a group produce an action plan time line, first clarify what decision the group decided to implement. Then ask the group to identify the actions needed to carry out the decision. Write down these actions on the flip chart. Once the group has agreed with the activities listed, ask them to sequence them so they can be listed according to what needs to be done first, second, third and so on. Next, ask for volunteers to take responsibility for carrying out each of the activities. Last, ask the volunteers to commit to a completion date for their action items.

Figure 6.12

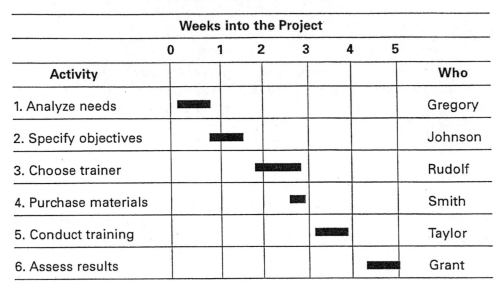

Action Plan Time Line

Weeks into the Project							
	0	1	2	3	4	5	
Activity							**Who**
1. Analyze needs	▬						Gregory
2. Specify objectives		▬					Johnson
3. Choose trainer			▬				Rudolf
4. Purchase materials			▪				Smith
5. Conduct training				▬			Taylor
6. Assess results					▬		Grant

Figure 6.12 is an example of an action plan time line. The project shown is a plan to train employees on newly purchased equipment. This is typically a very rewarding phase, since group members are able to witness the results of their efforts.

Chapter Summary

Tools for Organizational Improvement

PROBE is a flexible, straight-forward process model that can be used by groups to either solve business problems or address business opportunities. Business problems occur when something within the organization is not working in the correct manner, such as excessive errors, low productivity, or excessive complaints due to low customer satisfaction. Business opportunities are situations in which there isn't something wrong, but a decision needs to be made to take advantage of an observable opportunity. Examples of business opportunities are developing new product lines, increasing market share, looking for ways to stay ahead of the competition, or planning important events.

PROBE can be used by working exclusively in any of the specific phases, or beginning in the first phase, Projection, and moving through the entire model to the last phase, Execution. How much or how little of PROBE is used depends upon what the group is being asked to do.

How to Use PROBE

To use PROBE, first guide the group into the P step and help them develop a Projection for what is to be accomplished. Then, if the group is dealing with a problem, move them to the Root cause phase to analyze what is creating the problem. If dealing with an opportunity, skip over the Root cause phase. The next phase is called Options. This is where solutions or options are created by the group to reach its goal. After the options have been identified and organized, the group moves into the Best options phase to select the most viable options or solutions. Lastly, the Execution phase requires that the group develop a plan to implement the options selected.

Developing a Projection

To develop a projection, the group will need your help to create a goal statement. It should contain a measurable action to be taken, a list of the parameters the group must follow, and a description of how the organization will benefit.

Target the Root Cause

As the group's facilitator, you should only guide them into the Root cause phase only if the group is working to solve a problem, not if they are addressing an opportunity. You have a choice of three process tools in this phase — check sheet, flow chart and survey.

List the Options

Whether the group is solving a problem or addressing an opportunity, working in this phase affords them the choice of several process tools. You can help them build an initial list of options by using either brainstorm or round robin. Then ask them to clarify any items on the list that need clarification. Next, they should combine any similar items. Last, if necessary, they can categorize the list.

Choose the Best Options

You guide the group toward selecting the options that are the most viable in this phase. There are three tools to help you do this. First, use eliminate the obvious to cross off those options that definitely won't work, according to the group's opinion. Next, you can use multi-vote to pare down the list. With the remaining items, use compare against criteria to help the group make their final decision. Discussion is important in this phase and will help the group more easily reach a consensus.

Execute the Best Options

The final phase of PROBE is Execute best options. This is done with the use of an action plan time line. It helps the group implement the decisions made in the previous phase, Best options.

Using PROBE will help your groups follow an organized method to get things done. You need to educate them on how it works so they'll understand your recommendations. It won't be difficult convincing group members the importance of PROBE. This logical, structured approach will enable your groups to make a solid contribution to the business. Once they realize what they can accomplish using PROBE, they'll embrace it!

Should We Form a Team?

Albert: "Hold on a second. There's no way we can be expected to fix this problem. We don't have the budget and we surely don't have the time. Why can't they just hire someone to come in here and fix it? They're not going to agree with our solution, anyway!"

Michael: "I agree. This is a waste of our time!"

---

*I*f you were the facilitator of this group, you would probably be wishing you were somewhere else, rather than having to deal with these issues. However, there are some questions that have to be answered if this team is going to continue working on the project they've been assigned. These two team members need assurance that management will support them by supplying needed resources and backing up any solutions that are developed.

This chapter will address the issue of getting management support and how you can help what teams actually accomplish. Elements to consider when forming a team, the types of teams, and how teams work will also be discussed. Most importantly, the elements that build a successful team are identified. If you are involved in forming teams for either permanent or temporary purposes, this chapter explains how to do this effectively. As you read through these guidelines, you may find that the group you work with may not be called a team but exemplifies the characteristics being described. Use whatever information will help you make your group — or team — more effective.

What is a *team*? It is a group of people that work interdependently for a common purpose and are given the authority to solve problems and address opportunities within the organization. Often, groups who work together in this way don't call themselves a team. What members call themselves isn't important, as long as each individual is aware of how his or her contribution fits in with the group's overall objective.

There are many examples of how the team concept has been used for years in America, without anyone necessarily labeling group efforts as such. What did it take to get a man on the moon and safely back down again? How do presidential candidates win elections? How is it that some marriages strengthen and survive through years of adversity and challenge? We have all witnessed examples of superior teamwork in some aspect of our lives. Most of us were a part of a team experience at one time and have benefited from a successful teamwork initiative.

As a member of a tennis league in Atlanta called Atlanta Lawn Tennis Association (ALTA) since 1978, I have played on a number of different teams even winning the city championships several times. Some of the teams I played on were much more enjoyable than others. When team players practiced together regularly, and supported each other during competitive matches, the team was more cohesive. Teams like this stay together for years. Sooner or later, most people learn about the importance of creating cohesiveness when being involved in some type of team or group. Success on teams typically occurs when all individuals are willing to contribute equally and support each other fully.

Teams in Corporate America

One of the significant changes that has occurred in corporate America in the last 25 years has been the emergence of work teams. With the influence of such management gurus as W. Edwards Deming, who helped the Japanese rebuild following World War II, and the development of the Malcolm Baldridge National Quality Award in 1987, the emphasis on achieving quality through the use of work teams in business has become common.

More and more American companies are jumping on the bandwagon and implementing the work-team concept to improve their businesses. Look

around, and you will quickly see the formation of teams for both temporary purposes and long-term objectives. Often, these teams are not referred
to as teams, but as groups or some other name that describes what function is taking place. In spite of what teams are called, corporations are no
longer making all the decisions at the top — or so they would have you
believe. Decision-making authority is being pushed down to the levels
closest to the customer to create a greater sense of employee ownership
and commitment to the job.

Many companies are forming work teams for the first time, training
them inadequately or not at all, assigning facilitators, and then telling
the teams they're ready to go! When the groups fail, they blame the people involved, or the general team concept and not the real cause: the lack
of knowledge and skills needed to develop and manage a successful
team.

Enter the Facilitator

A competent, knowledgeable facilitator can make a gigantic difference in a
team's effectiveness. Even though the team itself is ultimately responsible
for the success of a project, the facilitator can guide a team toward cooper-
ation, improve communication between team members and top management, and ensure that the direction the team is going is really what each
team member believes to be the best option. Because facilitators focus on
how team members are working together, the facilitator can help educate
members on how they could work together more effectively.

A facilitator who doesn't understand his or her role can undermine the
success of a team. An incompetent facilitator could cause team members to
participate on a limited basis, prevent cohesive relationships among group
members, and create confusion over the team's objectives. Of all the functions necessary for a team to be successful, the training and education of
the facilitator is one of the most critical factors.

The Realities of Teams

When utilized properly, teams can accomplish much more than the sum of
its individual members. This is called *synergy* — the whole is greater than
the sum of its parts. Here are some general improvements that teams can
make and some related areas that teams focus on to accomplish the
improvements:

Increasing production:	Equipment downtime
	Maintenance delays
	Installation problems
	Shipment delays
	Customer service delays
	Slow cycle times
	Delayed patient care
	Untimely lab reports
Reducing errors:	Reports
	Billing
	Customer orders
	Supply quality
	Customer service needs
Eliminating waste:	Unnecessary procedures
	Excessive expenses
	Services not valued by the customer

There is no limit to what a team can accomplish. However, there are some guidelines that should be considered to determine when or if a team is needed.

Work teams can be effective provided they are utilized in the right circumstances. Before organizing a team, consider the following points:

- There should be enough time to allow a team to work effectively on an issue.
- The specific business issue or problem should have more than one possible solution.
- The project should be too large in scope for any one person to accomplish it.
- Management should be committed to the successful achievement of the goal.

Just as there is an ideal set of circumstances for organizing a team, there are also instances in which the organization of a team is inappropriate. A work team is not needed:

- Just because using teams is the latest management technique.
- When the issue at hand is more suited to the control or expertise of one person.
- When you have already decided on a solution to a particular problem and just want group commitment.
- When you are facing an emergency with a short time frame.

The consequences of using a team when one is not really needed can be devastating, even if not immediately visible. For example, imagine that a customer service manager has selected a new headpiece for his customer service representatives to use. He found what he was looking for and it fit into the department budget. However, he wanted to get the new headpiece "blessed" by his CSRs, so he called a meeting. At the beginning of the meeting he told CSRs that they would be deciding on whether to purchase the headpiece he had been considering. The CSRs didn't like his choice, and actually found another model that they preferred, even though it was more expensive. The manager decided to stay with his original choice. If this example had actually happened, the CSRs would end up resenting his decision because they'd realize that he was sticking with his selection, whether they agreed with that choice or not. They would wonder why he even bothered to ask them their opinion in the first place. The manager would suffer a loss of credibility and create a situation that encourages CSRs to continue to complain about the new equipment.

I hear this type of complaint from team members all the time, in almost every company I work with. Rather than asking for a team opinion, members reason, a manager should present his or her decision and explain why it is the best option available. In other words, don't ask for input when you don't really want to hear it.

There are two types of teams; permanent and temporary. Each is appropriate in different situations, based upon the environment and the nature of the desired objective.

A permanent team contains members who work together on an ongoing basis. For example, a team of power plant employees might have the permanent responsibility of monitoring and improving the performance of the plant's equipment.

A temporary team contains members who are brought together for a specific purpose or project — an effort that has a beginning and an end. When the project is over, the team members go their separate ways. An example of a temporary team is one brought together to create a more user-friendly billing system.

Whether they are permanent or temporary, team members can be either *functional, cross-functional,* or *multi-functional.* Functional teams consist of individuals who hold the same job title and possess similar job skills. They often work in the same area, are assigned to one portion of a work procedure, and perform the same tasks. For example, since a payroll procedure can be a complex process in a large company, there are typically several employees assigned to key in weekly wages and generate checks. When brought together as a team, they could be asked to assist one another or to improve their work procedures. Another example of a functional team might be a group of cable technicians assigned the task of reducing reworks on service calls.

Cross-functional teams are made up of individuals who are assigned to different departments and have different skills and different jobs, but who contribute to the same work procedure. An example would be a team formed to reduce errors in its billing system. In a typical organization, several people in various departments work on different aspects of the billing system, so it would be appropriate to form a team with members who contribute to different portions of billing. Team members might include the telephone service representative who initiates an invoice after a customer calls to place an order, or the service representative who fills the order. Another likely team member could be the accounting manager who generates the actual invoice that is mailed to the customer. Those who could contribute to good customer service as it relates to billing would make qualified team members. Cross-functional teams are effective when a company wants to improve an entire work procedure by increasing productivity, improving quality or eliminating waste across departments.

A cross-functional team could also be comprised of members of the same department who contribute to the same work process, but perform different tasks and responsibilities. Since they do not all have the same knowledge, when one person goes on vacation, that particular person's work does not get done. In this way, cross-functional teams are often at a disadvantage. Because of this, many companies today are striving to train all cross-functional employees to perform all the varied tasks carried out in a particular department. When this occurs, the team becomes multi-functional.

Multi-functional teams are made up of team members who individually possess all of the skills required to complete an entire work procedure.

Multi-functional team members have been trained to perform all functions of a work procedure. One example of this is contract administrators. There is usually a long process used by large companies to develop, initiate, monitor, and enforce contracts with suppliers. Since each team member understands how to perform all the job functions associated with contract administration, individuals work together closely. Employees provide support to one another when needed, even though they each have their own contract assignments. This type of team is very versatile because each member can perform all of the work functions in one entire work procedure. When one team member is on vacation, his or her responsibilities are still carried out, since all team members have the knowledge to perform all positions in their work area.

What do teams actually focus on? The typical corporate environment is made of up *internal* and *external suppliers*, and *internal* and *external customers*. The typical work team is brought together for the purpose of managing the system between the supplier and customer. Figure 7.1 illustrates the relationship between suppliers, teams and customers.

The term *internal* refers to entities inside the organization, and the word *external* refers to those that are outside. A supplier provides the work team goods and services needed to perform a function. The team prepares these goods and services for use by the customer. An internal supplier might be the warehouse employee who provides technicians with the equipment they need to provide service to their customers. In this example, the equipment provided by the warehouse staff must be in good working order, must be delivered on time, and must be the exact specifications required by the technicians.

An external supplier might be a contract employee who doesn't work for the organization, who is utilized when there is a labor shortage, or when a

---

Figure 7.1

The Supplier, Team, and Customer Relationship

Suppliers ⟶ Work Team ⟶ Customers

Managing
the
System

specialized need arises. The labor (or product) provided by the contractor must meet the organization's requirements also.

An internal customer is an employee of the company who is a recipient of goods or services being provided by someone else who is an employee of the company. Just as the warehouse associate in the previous example is an internal supplier for the technicians, the technician is an internal customer for the warehouse associate. Who is the external customer in this example? The consumer who does not work for the organization and is the recipient of the service installation provided by the technician.

In between the *input* that is being received by the supplier, and the *output* that is being received by the customer, there is a function called system management that ensures that there is desired quality and productivity. Work teams manage this system and ensure that it performs at optimum levels. Much of this work is done using the process model discussed in Chapter 6: PROBE.

How the Facilitator Helps

In order to ensure the success of a team, you should attend to certain key areas. As the facilitator, you must interface with team members, suppliers, customers, and management whenever a new project is assigned to the team, or whenever the team recognizes a new business need. There are several important guidelines to fulfill.

First, develop a written statement that identifies the problem, purpose or need for a team. You should include the following elements: clear definition of the problem or need; a description of the expected business payoff; and an estimate of the resources and time frame required.

Next, present the formal recommendation to management for approval. Identify management restrictions, determine how management wants to remain informed of the team's progress and clarify how much authority the team has.

There are three levels of authority a team can receive. It is very important that a team understands its level, so that members can work comfortably within the boundaries. As the facilitator, you should discuss the team's authority level with management to help management decide and verbalize just how far the team can go. These levels are established on a project-by-project basis, or one level is established for all projects assigned to a particular team.

The first level of authority is called Level 1: Full Empowerment or post-updating. This level is present when the team has full decision making authority in reaching the established goal and updates the boss as decisions are carried out.

As an example, imagine that a team is charged with eliminating all mechanical failures in its vehicle maintenance program. The team has the authority to do whatever is necessary to make this happen, with no approval from anyone. It must stay within its current departmental budget, but the group has full authority in deciding how it will reach this objective. It must keep upper management updated on current activity, but can go ahead with any decision made without management approval.

Years ago, I managed a group of trainers in human resources at Food Giant, Inc. The level of authority I assigned this group was full empowerment. They kept me informed, but they did whatever they felt was needed to train all the hourly employees in the retail supermarkets. They decided they wanted to reinforce all of the training skills that were being taught at the time, so they designed a company-wide game, called Customer Pursuit. There were competitions in each store, then store winners went to district competitions. There was eventually a final corporate competition in which the winners were given a vacation trip for two. Not only did my trainers reinforce the learning principles that were taught in the training programs, they also sent the message that learning can be fun. The whole project was hatched, designed and implemented by the trainers, not by myself. Yet, my contribution was allowing them to do what they felt was necessary. This is an example of how Level 1 allows a group to make a significant impact on the welfare of an organization.

The second level of authority is called Level 2: Management Approval or pre-approval. This second level occurs when the team presents its recommendations for management approval after it has made a decision, and waits for a response before carrying out any plans. Using the previous example of teams trying to eliminate mechanical failures, Level 2 requires that the team present its recommendation for improvement to management. Management will review the recommendation and give the team authority to implement its recommendation, or possibly negotiate changes in the plan.

The third level of authority is called Level 3: Management Decision or no authority. In this situation, the team presents ideas for management to consider; it does not make the final decision. At this level, the team has virtually no authority. It simply presents its ideas to management. Management can either implement the team's plan, or choose another course of action. This is the least desirable level of empowerment for a team. As the facilitator, you should try to convince management to avoid this mode, because it limits the amount of ownership and commitment team members experience, therefore negating one of the important benefits that comes from the presence of work teams: ownership and dedication to the business.

Once the levels of authority are established, the next step is to identify the parameters. First of all, get approval for the resources the team needs, such as the number of people needed to work on the team, the necessary budget to achieve the goal, and any equipment needed to carry out the team's objective. Next, negotiate the schedule, including deadlines, for the successful completion of the team's objective. An agreement on how much the team must produce to justify its existence is also important, as well as a description of the specific area the team must focus on.

If you are forming a new team, the structure of it needs to be defined. This is done after approval for forming the team is received. Plans should be made for how the team will be organized if it is coming together for the first time. Determine the following functions:

- Identify to whom the team will report
- Identify influential people who give support to the group
- Identify stakeholders: those who are affected by the team's decisions and need to be kept informed
- Develop a plan for selecting team members
- Identify roles, responsibilities, and qualifications of the team members
- Decide who will educate, coach, and train the team if and when needed

Keep in mind that the optimum number of team members on any given team is six to twelve people. The team may limit its creativity with a smaller number, or become too difficult to work with in the case of a larger number.

The Initial Team Planning Form, shown in Figure 7.2, can be used to assist you in organizing a new team. This can also be used to organize and publish the necessary information to keep appropriate people informed.

Team Development Stages

Once a temporary or permanent team has been formed, and is working on its first project, it will develop and grow through four different stages:

Figure 7.2

Initial Team Planning Form

Use this planner for new team projects, or for newly developed teams.

1. Specific problem/need _____

_____

2. Customer needs related to this situation _____

_____

3. Expected business payoff _____

_____

4. Appropriate empowerment level: Level 1 (Post-updating)

Level 2 (Pre-approval)

Level 3 (None)

_____

5. Team structure: Facilitator _____

Reports to _____

Team member responsibilities _____

_____

Selection process to begin on: _____ First group meeting_____

Team member qualifications _____

Those who can give support _____

Stakeholders to be kept informed _____

Trainer/coach for the group _____

Project deadline _____

How often team will meet _____

1. Forming
2. Storming
3. Norming
4. Performing

The facilitator must understand each of the four phases and be able to identify which phase a team is in. Once a particular phase of growth has been identified, the facilitator can then help the team be more effective in that particular stage. These stages should be used as a guide, since every team or group does not fit into a predictable pattern. Team members often find themselves going through the stages of development at different times. In other words, a team that has moved into the performing phase might still return to the storming phase at times.

The *forming* phase occurs as team members get to know one another and bond with one another. Individuals react quite differently from each other in this phase. Some are very eager to jump into the project, while others take a more reluctant approach. Usually team members display an initial "politeness" with one another. As the team begins to work together, things may appear to be progressing quite nicely. Initial friendships that form often are positive, and the team performs fairly well at this stage. This atmosphere usually changes as the team members work together more extensively and the "newness" of the situation wears off.

What can the facilitator do to help a team in the forming stage? The facilitator must help the team get past the initial politeness and discomfort that exists in a new environment. This will clear the way for more serious issues to surface. The facilitator should help the team clarify sources of discomfort by asking questions. For example, "I noticed some head-shaking when we discussed what our time frame should be for this project. Do we need to discuss the deadline further?"

During forming, team members may also tend to focus on one another's differences without recognizing how to capitalize on them. The facilitator can encourage the team to use its diversity to its advantage. Teams must utilize all members to reach their full potential. In addition, the facilitator can point out the common goal that members have and ask them how they plan to work with their differences. The facilitator might say, "This team represents a lot of diverse talent, which will be particularly helpful in reaching our objective of increasing revenue opportunities with our new product. What are your suggestions for fully utilizing the talent in this room?"

As the team develops, members move into the *storming* phase. Due to disagreements and disparities regarding how the team is operating, conflict arises. Teams don't always deal with this effectively. Conflict and disagreement are allowed to surface and be resolved — and the facilitator can help make this happen. Chapter 5 discusses how groups or teams deal with conflict, and how the facilitator helps manage it.

A team must go through this storming phase in order to continue to grow and develop. Conflict usually occurs early on because the team has not yet had an opportunity to reach a consensus on the best ways to work together. Conflict areas provide the team with opportunities to decide how to work together effectively and move to the next phase. As differences and tensions surface, the facilitator should allow and encourage discussion of these differences. If the discussion becomes destructive, with team members making personal attacks, the facilitator should step in and remind the group that this is not acceptable. They are then encouraged to focus on the issues, not the people. The group will move through the storming phase only if the facilitator constantly encourages a discussion of the issues. "Let's remember that we're discussing how these errors occurred and what can be done to prevent them. We've agreed that personal attacks are not constructive, and certainly won't help anyone reach an agreement on this issue. Lynn, continue explaining your plan for correcting this problem ..."

In the *norming* phase, the team begins to experience authentic success in working toward its objectives. They have identified behaviors that, if displayed consistently, help members work together effectively. These accepted behaviors, called *group norms*, have been discovered as a result of the difficulties experienced in phase two. Team members have learned what works best for them. Examples of group norms are:

- No interrupting when another person is talking. If it occurs, the person talking has the right to remind the interrupter of the rule.
- No criticizing of those who disagree with the majority. Give dissenters a chance to express their views, hear them out, then strive for consensus.
- Silence means consent. If someone doesn't speak out against an idea, it will be assumed that everyone agrees with it.
- Make a concerted effort to listen and understand other's ideas, even if you don't agree.
- Stay on schedule — finish projects within the agreed upon time frame.

There are two types of norms that emerge in this phase: *inherent* norms and *overt* norms. Inherent norms are natural behavior tendencies that occur automatically and help the team maintain its effectiveness. Overt norms are behaviors that the team learns. Not all norms are positive, but team members should work toward focusing on the positive norms and avoiding the ones that make it difficult for them to be successful together. Inherent and overt norms that are positive should be put into practice once group members recognize that they will help the team be more effective.

In order to help the team recognize the most effective means of working together, the facilitator should point out both the inherent and overt norms of behavior that seem to work well or are needed. Praising the team's productiveness and encouraging the team to solve problems when difficulties do arise will help the team become more independent. The facilitator should challenge team members to rely on themselves to accomplish goals, work out conflicts, and become a cohesive unit.

The Team Mission/Objective form in Figure 7.3 is used to help develop positive, overt norms by clarifying why the team exists, what it's

---

Figure 7.3

Team Mission/Objectives Form

1. Who are our customers?

2. Who are our suppliers

3. Why does our team exist?

4. How do we contribute to our company's mission and vision?

5. What specific tasks are we responsible for?

6. What authority level do we have?

7. What are our ground rules for working together effectively?

8. What are our ground rules for resolving conflict?

9. What are our ground rules for length, frequency, and location of our meetings?

---

responsible for, and how they will work together. A facilitator can use this form to help a group reach an agreement on these elements.

The *performing* phase is the ultimate development phase for a team. This phase is characterized by rapport and strong bonds among team members. All team members stand ready and willing to help one another in reaching team objectives. The team is very independent, and it responds automatically to any challenges or issues that arise.

A mature, performing team can accomplish quite a bit. It has experienced conflict and knows how to manage it. Team members have made commitments on how they will support each other and work together, and consistently adhere to these commitments. Teams in this phase have a great sense of pride in what they have accomplished and in their potential for future success.

The facilitator should serve as the catalyst for movement toward continuous improvement for a performing team. Since the team members share a common vision in this phase, they will be able to initiate many of their own projects based upon priorities. The facilitator becomes the team's advisor by pointing out areas where additional improvements in the process could be made. Since the performing team experiences a large amount of success, the facilitator has many opportunities to encourage members, reinforce a job well done, and praise the group.

Chapter Summary

Helping Teams Be Successful

This chapter has identified how to form a team and create an environment that helps a team maintain success. Remember that often team members refer to themselves as groups, but it doesn't matter what members call themselves. The definition of a team is a group of people that work together and who are given the authority to solve problems and address opportunities in the business. Some groups are labeled "teams" but really don't have any authority. The facilitator helps in clarifying exactly what the team can and cannot do.

The Realities of Teams

Teams work on increasing production, reducing errors and eliminating waste. They should be brought together when the situation requires more than one person, contains more than one possible solution, and allows enough time for the team to address it. A team should not be involved when management is simply trying to get a group to "bless" a decision that was already made. This creates a lack of credibility between management and the team.

There are two types of teams — permanent teams, which have been created for an indefinite amount of time, and temporary teams, which are created to work on special projects that have a beginning date and an ending date. Team members can be functional (same job, similar skills), cross-functional (different skills and jobs, same work process), and multi-functional (same skills, all know all steps of a work process).

Teams work by managing a system for quality and productivity and providing supplies for both internal and external customers. Teams also have their own internal and external suppliers that provide the materials needed to manage a system effectively.

How the Facilitator Helps

The facilitator helps teams perform in a number of ways. He or she develops written statements to identify the objective, the business payoff and the estimate of resources. The facilitator also clarifies which level of empowerment the team is being assigned; Level 1, 2, or 3. The facilitator is responsible for acquiring the needed resources, the necessary budget and negotiation of deadlines for accomplishing the specified goal. The Initial Team Planning Form is a good tool for identifying what needs to be done.

Team Development Stages

The facilitator helps the team grow and develop through the four stages of team growth. Team members need to be candid and learn to value each other's differences in the forming stage. Conflict and disagreement should be allowed to surface in the storming stage. The facilitator should help the team identify the most appropriate behaviors for success in the norming stage. This allows the group to identify positive group norms for members to practice. The Team Mission/Objective Form is a good tool for clarifying these norms. For a performing team, the facilitator serves as a catalyst for continued improvement.

The dynamics that take place in a team or group are usually not predictable. If you have an opportunity to work with several different teams, you'll find that no two teams are alike. But, this chapter gives you information that will help you understand the general principles of team dynamics, so you can be a more effective facilitator.

What Do I Do Now?

N ow that you have read about the skills needed for managing a meeting and a group, it's time to apply them to the real-life scenarios described in this chaper.

How would you handle each of these difficult situations if you were the facilitator? First, write your answer on a separate sheet of paper. Then, review the appropriate response following each of these cases.

Case One

You are facilitating a group of managers for a major automobile manufacturer. Jim has brought up an important issue — how to improve production time. Members are trying to estimate how much production time can be decreased for each of the alternatives they are considering. Mary introduces a new subject, the design for one of next year's models, and wants to discuss it in detail.

Case One Response

As the facilitator, you should ask Mary if the new subject could be listed on the parking lot sheet, to be addressed later. You might say, "Right now, we're discussing ways to improve production time. In order to stay focused, could we add this new subject to the parking lot to be addressed later?"

Remember, the parking lot is a posted list of topics mentioned during the meeting that are not part of the intended meeting agenda. These topics can be discussed at another point during the meeting, or after the session, whichever is most appropriate. You may need to ask members if they want to add the subject to the meeting agenda at the most logical point of that day's discussion, or if they would like to discuss it at another meeting. Sometimes a subject requires that you do some research before the group discusses the issue. Such topics would need to be addressed at another meeting. Additionally, after asking if the topic should be added to the parking lot, Mary may indicate that it isn't necessary — she simply got carried away.

Case Two

You are working with a group of information technology support managers from a medium size long distance company. They are clarifying a list of options on how to add value to their internal customers. As group members begin to clarify the list that has just been created, Delores, a very persuasive team member, begins to discuss how well the fifth option would work. She likes this option because several of her customers have recommended it.

Case Two Response

You should ask Delores to hold her comments until after the group has finished clarifying all of the options. "Delores, could you please hold your comments about that? Let's finish clarifying these options to make sure everyone understands them. Then, I'll come back to you when we start evaluating." Then don't forget to get back to Delores!

Case Three

You are facilitating a group from a lending institution that is discussing how to introduce a new equity accelerator program. Your group consists of several members with different job positions, representing a cross-section of bank employees. Nato, a loan officer, makes a suggestion that no one else in the group acknowledges. You sense that the rest of the group doesn't like the idea.

Case Three Response

Allow all suggestions to be addressed, even if the group doesn't like a particular idea. Offer specific guidance. "What about Nato's suggestion?

What are your thoughts?" Help the group fully consider all suggestions, before it determines which options are best. You also protect the self-esteem of group members by ensuring that all ideas are heard. This encourages participation from all members.

Case Four

A group of retail store managers is planning a big product promotion for an upcoming holiday. James is discussing an idea he has, but is interrupted by Joey who enthusiastically jumps into the discussion.

Case Four Response

When one group member interrupts another, simply say, "Joey, hold on — let's wait for James to finish and we'll hear your comment next." It is common for group members to interrupt each other. By reminding them to listen to the entire message before interrupting, you set a precedent for good communication skills among group members. You also encourage members to stay involved in the conversation. Do not forget to get Joey's input next.

Case Five

Your group is from a brokerage company and they are brainstorming ideas for a new financial product. There is a lot of energy and excitement during this portion of the meeting. Two people, Annette and Nick, start talking at the same time. Annette "wins out" and is able to thoroughly discuss her idea.

Case Five Response

After Annette is finished, go to Nick, who started to talk, but did not get a chance to share his views, "Nick, did you start to say something?" Some group members will not offer a comment after being cut off. You can provide encouragement by calling on those who want to say something, but need an opening in the conversation to do so.

Case Six

You are facilitating a group from a small accounting firm. They are planning a retirement party for one of their senior members. Nina is explaining her suggestion to the rest of the group. She talks for quite some time and appears to be rambling. You notice that some of the other group members, especially Rita and Michael are becoming impatient and are ready to move on.

Case Six Response

When she takes a breath or pauses, try paraphrasing what she has said, then check to be sure the group understands what she is saying. "So what you're saying is … Is that right? Good. Does everyone understand what Nina is saying? Then are we ready to move on?" Group members sometimes need help in expressing themselves. If you are effectively listening, you can draw out the ideas being expressed so that everyone is understood.

Case Seven

You work with a children's hospital. The meeting you are facilitating involves a group of human resources specialists. They are creating a plan for rolling out a new training program the hospital has purchased. As the group is discussing an issue, a sidebar conversation begins between Frank and Rebecca. It is distracting to the rest of the group, but the two group members are not aware of this.

Case Seven Response

Whenever there is a prolonged sidebar conversation in which a smaller group begins to discuss matters on their own, you should address it immediately and tactfully by saying something like, "Let's remember to focus on what's going on so we don't miss anything." If the sidebar continues, intervene by talking to the individuals privately during a break. "I'm noticing that you are having a number of sidebar conversations. Have either of you noticed this?" Give them time to discuss it. Then ask, "What impact is this having on you?" If they cannot answer this question, explain that private conversations can be distracting for the group, and this behavior casts a shadow of doubt on their level of commitment to the project. Then ask, "What can you do to avoid these sidebar conversations?" Be ready to offer a suggestion, such as having Frank and Rebecca sit in opposite corners of the room.

Case Eight

You are facilitating a group of high school principles. They are working on ideas for a new curriculum focusing on history. Connie is making a suggestion and is having trouble expressing her thoughts accurately — she is searching for the right words. Bob tries to help by rephrasing the suggestion.

Case Eight Response

Make sure that Bob, who is trying to help, is accurately rephrasing the other person's message. Ask Connie, the group member who initially made the suggestion, "Connie, is that what you were saying?" It is important to capture the exact thoughts of the person contributing the idea so there is no misunderstanding about what the person wants to say.

Case Nine

You are working with a group of engineers from a gas company. The group is 20 minutes into the meeting. You notice that there are two silent members, Lynn and Alberta, that haven't said anything yet.

Case Nine Response

Pull in silent members tactfully and gently. "Let's hear from someone who has not had a chance to express their opinion on this. Do you have anything to add?"

If this doesn't help, then you can directly ask a silent member, "Lynn, have you had a chance to formulate an opinion yet?"

Silent group members may have a number of reasons for being silent. They could have serious concerns about the topic being discussed, or they may not have formed an opinion yet. Sometimes members are naturally quiet and introverted. It is important to ask for their involvement tactfully, so they are not singled out.

Case Ten

There is a group of automobile dealers that has met three times. They are sharing ideas on how to create loyalty in customers. You notice that there is one person, Pete, who never speaks or contributes any ideas. You've called on him a few times to ask for his input, but he never has anything to say.

Case Ten Response

Since you have already called on Pete several times during the group meetings and he is still not participating, it is time to do an intervention to change behavior. In other words, talk to him during the break or outside the meeting in private. "Pete, you are silent most of the time during meetings. Are you conscious of this, or are you normally quiet?" Give him time to express his views. Then ask, "How do you think this impacts you?" If he doesn't know, explain that the group is missing out on his expertise and may perceive that he is uninterested in the project. Next, you should ask Pete, "What could you do to be more active and involved?" If Pete doesn't have any ideas, be prepared to offer your own. "If we are discussing an area that you know something about, just raise your hand and I'll make sure you have a chance to contribute. I'll also be calling on you more often to give you more opportunities to speak." You have now discussed the situation with Pete and have clearly told him you expect him to participate more.

Case Eleven

You are facilitating a group of corporate lawyers who work for a large telecommunications company. You notice that there is one group member, Rita, who is doing all the talking during the meeting. She is monopolizing the discussion by clarifying continuously.

Case Eleven Response

This is challenging: the dominating, overly-vocal individual! Rita cannot be ignored because, the problem will reflect on you if it is not handled. First try to be subtle and make broad statements to pull in other people, such as, "Well, we heard from Rita. Let's hear from someone else. What are your ideas about this?"

If Rita does not "take the hint" after you have tried this a few times, then you must talk to her privately and make an intervention. Tell her, "Rita, your enthusiasm sometimes prevents others from contributing their ideas. Have you noticed that you tend to spend a lot of time giving your ideas?" Give her time to discuss her views, then ask, "How do you think this is impacting you?"

If she doesn't know, tell her, "It seems that group members resist your ideas because you contribute to such a great degree. What could you do to make it easier for the other group members to participate?"

If she doesn't have any suggestions, offer yours. "State your ideas after you have given others a chance to speak. You might even consider being silent more often."

Case Twelve

A group of customer service managers is trying to identify performance standards for their customer service reps in a call center. You were facilitating their discussion. There seem to be two opposing viewpoints. Sheila, Ron, Laura, and Sarah think that the reps should be able to handle at least 50 calls per day. Jay, John, Matt and Jessica believe the reps should be encouraged to spend more time with each caller, thereby reducing the daily number of calls to only 35. They debated this subject for 20 minutes.

Case Twelve Response

First of all, remind the group of the amount of time that has been allotted for the meeting, and what has been planned for the rest of the agenda. Ask members if they want to continue discussing this issue, or think about it and address it later. If the group decides to continue discussing it, intervene by listing the opposing points of view in outline form on the easel. Then ask the group members to point out areas of agreement and disagreement, as you write them on the flip chart. You can then ask them to develop a solution that could be supported by all.

Case Thirteen

You have been facilitating a group who works in a power plant. The meeting has been in session for one hour. The group members are trying to develop a plan for outages. You have a group member, John, who falls asleep.

Case Thirteen Response

If a group member is sleeping, call a break. He or she may just need a cup of coffee or a soda. If the problem continues, address it one-on-one and find out why the person is sleeping.

"John, you are the subject-matter expert on this project. You have the knowledge and experience that the group needs. When you fall asleep, this gives the group the impression that you simply don't care about the project. I'd like to discuss why you're sleeping, and what can be done to keep you awake." Be ready to suggest that he drink coffee, or stand up in the back of the room when he gets sleepy, if he cannot think of any solutions. If he is able to explain why he is falling asleep, this could give you some additional ideas on how to help him solve the problem.

This is one way to make an intervention to change behavior. As you get more comfortable as a facilitator, you will find other methods that are equally effective. Remember to focus on behavior, get to the point, and validate the person's strengths.

Case Fourteen

You are facilitating a team of salespeople in a software company. They are charged with identifying prospective customers in new markets. Team members have indicated that they don't want to be a team. Several members, including Elizabeth, Angelique, Thomas, and Rick do not feel that the company has demonstrated real support for their efforts.

Case Fourteen Response

Ask members why they feel this way. Build a list of actions management could take to give the group support. Offer to present it to management, or ask members if they would like to select someone from the team to present it. If the team does not want to approach management, then encourage members to list ways they can operate, given the current situation. If this does not work, then you might consider sitting down and talking to management about the situation. Bring a recommendation for resolving the issue.

The discussion with management should go something like this: "This team has a lot of talent and initiative, so they will require little supervision on this project. However, they feel that they are not getting the outside support they need to get the job done effectively. I suggest you meet with the members and hear what their needs are for this project. Once they understand that they have the support they need, they will be able to refocus their energies to meet their objectives. How does this sound to you?"

Case Fifteen

You are facilitating a meeting for a group of district managers who work for a grocery chain. They are forecasting sales for the upcoming quarter.

The group's manager, Vince, is dominating the group and taking too much control of the discussion.

Case Fifteen Response

Even bosses and managers need feedback, but it should be offered in private. You might ask Vince to limit his comments so that the group does not feel pressure to follow his lead, since the purpose of the meeting is to gain input from the district managers. You might say, "It's clear this issue is important to you, and your belief in the project is important to the group. However, your involvement in the discussion makes it difficult for the rest of the group members to participate. They become more hesitant. What can you do to show your enthusiasm, and still allow group members to contribute?"

If Vince has no ideas, tell him, "I suggest you refrain from contributing your opinions. Simply praise the group for their hard work, and support them by offering whatever they need to accomplish their task."

Summary

After reading this book, you've reviewed how to manage a team's meeting to ensure that all the necessary elements are in place. This provides the structure a team or group needs. You've discovered the importance of maintaining neutrality so that ownership is allowed to develop within the group. Techniques for getting group members fully engaged and helping a group address their disagreements have been discussed. This ensures that all member's views are heard and understood. You've received many tools for making organizational improvements, as well.

By following these guidelines, you will create a structured, comfortable, and motivating environment for your groups, virtually every time. Team members will respond by being fully engaged, enthusiastic, and fully committed. You'll be the catalyst as they whole-heartedly make the decisions, implement them and move the organization toward meaningful change.

The Case of Cable Express, Inc.

*Y*ou've now read about all the principles for conducting effective meetings, solving problems, and leading groups in an organized manner toward their objectives for improving organizations. You've also evaluated situations that typically arise for facilitators. Hopefully, you have already begun to put these principles into action.

This chapter will give you an opportunity to review these principles. You will be reading about a fictitious cable company called Cable Express. The company has a few operational problems that are impacting its customers. You will see how a facilitator might typically help a management team choose the most pressing problem to focus on first, then define the problem, identify the root cause of the problem and develop options for solving the problem.

Cable Express, Inc.

Cable Express (CE) is a cable company with 45,000 residential customers. CE is based in a large city and is one of four cable companies that serve the city. CE is a medium-sized company compared to the others in this market, but it is part of a nationwide cable organization with operations in 15 other states in the nation.

While Cable Express is backed by a large and successful parent company, all the company-owned systems are held to very stringent budgets. So resources, at times, can be limited. When extra funding is needed, it has to be approved by the home office.

Cable Express has been experiencing several problems in its operations recently. First, the company has been losing customers in a few areas. A competing cable company (owned by a telecommunications firm) has begun sending out door-to-door salespeople who are able to hook up cable instantly. Although this has only occurred in a few of CE's outlying areas, the company has lost approximately 45 percent of its customers in these markets. Several customers who decided to go with the competition stated that they were tired of waiting for Cable Express to hook them up. This is understandable, since CE customers currently experience a four day wait. There have also been problems for existing customers who order additional services or request repair work. The waiting time is even longer than it is for new customers — seven days. There have also been a very large number of customer complaints, focusing on some common issues such as billing errors, rude customer service reps and poor quality pictures after cable has been installed.

After meeting with his management team to discuss the issues, the general manager at CE, John Duffy, realizes his company needs the expertise of a facilitator to help them acquire some focus around solving some of the problems discussed. He meets with several potential facilitators and decides on Natalie Simonson.

The First Meeting

In preparing for the first meeting, Natalie realizes from the initial discussion with John Duffy that there are several problems at CE. She knows that an organization with limited resources should focus on one major area at a time. Often this will result in other problems or issues being resolved and it helps focus employees on one area. They experience results faster and are then motivated to tackle another area. So, she develops the following outcome: A prioritized list of CE problems that need to be solved. Once this list is developed by the group they can tackle each problem, one at a time.

Now, Natalie is ready to develop the agenda. Figure A.1 illustrates the developed agenda. During the "Beginning of the Meeting" phase, Natalie plans time in the agenda for the group to develop their own list of ground rules, since they will be meeting on an ongoing basis. Natalie contracts with the group by asking if everyone is willing to follow these ground rules for each of the meetings they will be attending.

Figure A.1

Meeting Agenda for Cable Express
First Meeting

Expected Outcome: A prioritized list of CE problems to solve

Date: January 5

Time: 9:00 A.M.

Place: Conference room

Who Should Attend: F. Catalfamo, J. Duffy, A. Franklin, T. Hoff, L. King, M. Kensey, L. Little, B. Moss, J. Mewing, L. Palma, R. Polly, R. Ringer

What	Time	Who
Beginning of the Meeting		
1. Welcome the group	5 minutes	
2. Clarify the outcome	5 minutes	
3. Set role expectations	5 minutes	
4. Establish ground rules		
a. Brainstorm a list of ground rules		
b. Clarify the list		
c. Contract with the group	20 minutes	
5. Discuss agenda	5 minutes	
Body of the Meeting		
6. Brainstorm a list of problems	15 minutes	
7. Clarify the problems that need further explanation	10 minutes	
8. Prioritize the list using multi-vote	15 minutes	
9. Verify the first problem to work on	5 minutes	
End of the Meeting		
10. Summarize against the outcome	1 minute	
11. Verify action items, set next meeting date	1 minute	
12. Praise the group's effort	1 minute	

For the "Body of the Meeting, she decides to use a portion of the PROBE process model — the O and B steps. Natalie plans to facilitate as the group brainstorms a list of current problems that CE is experiencing. Then the problems that need clarification will be discussed to ensure everyone understands them. Lastly, the group will use the multi-vote process tool to prioritize the list from most important to least important. To review any of the process tools mentioned here, look at Chapter 6.

Natalie will end the meeting by summarizing, setting the next meeting date and verifying any other action items that need discussion. She will close the meeting on a positive note by praising the group members on something they did that was especially effective.

After looking over the agenda she has developed, Natalie plans the meeting for approximately one and one half hours. This will give the group ample time to achieve the intended outcome. Natalie is anticipating the group will have questions since this is their first meeting with her. One and a half hours should be plenty of time to achieve the outcome and answer any questions. This agenda is for Natalie's eyes only, (it has more detail than the group needs), so she will publish another agenda that has less detail and sends it out to the group in advance of the meeting. Figure A.2 shows the agenda group members will be using.

At the meeting, unnecessary truck rolls becomes the number one priority on the list. A truck roll occurs whenever a technician drives from the warehouse to a customer's house to perform service. An unnecessary truck roll occurs if a technician makes more than one trip to the customer's home when the service could have been provided in only one trip. The company's key measurements concerning truck rolls indicate that each day, approximately 150 customers are visited by 13 technicians. There are 40 unnecessary visits back to the warehouse and then back again to the customer's house, so instead of 150 visits, there are 190 visits. That means that 21 percent of the truck rolls are unnecessary. By solving this one problem, the managers realize that they could dramatically reduce the amount of time it takes to hook up new customers and provide service for existing customers. This would reduce the amount of complaints they are getting about delayed service.

The Second Meeting

Now, Natalie is ready to prepare for her second meeting. She will apply the PROBE model to the problem of unnecessary truck rolls, which the

Figure A.2

CE Agenda for Group Members to Use

Expected Outcome: A prioritized list of CE problems to solve

Date: January 5

Time: 9:00 A.M.

Place: Conference room

Who Should Attend: F. Catalfamo, J. Duffy, A. Franklin, T. Hoff, L. King, M. Kensey, L. Little, B. Moss, J. Mewing, L. Palma, R. Polly, R. Ringer

What	Time	Who
Introduction	7 minutes	
Outcome		
Set role expectations		
Establish ground rules		
Brainstorm a list of ground rules	10 minutes	
Clarify the list		
Contract with the group		
Brainstorm a list of problems	15 minutes	
Clarify the problems	10 minutes	
Prioritize the list using multi-vote and choose one problem to work on	20 minutes	
Summarize, set next meeting date	3 minutes	

management team decided is its first priority (from the first meeting). The second session will require more thought and preparation from Natalie. The group will begin with the P or projection phase, which means they'll create a goal that defines the problem and describes to what extent the problem will be solved.

As part of the preparation phase, Natalie also needs to choose which tool from the R or Root Cause phase is most appropriate. Since the problem is unnecessary truck rolls, it is important to find out what is causing this. There are probably several factors, so a check sheet would be a good way to track both the causes and the number of occurrences. The group may also later want to examine the entire work process beginning with the customer placing a telephone order to a customer service representative and ending with the technician appearing at the customer's home to handle the order. A flow chart would be used for this analysis. Since it would be very involved, and it might dilute both the company resources and the group focus, the Natalie decides to stick to the check sheet for now.

So, Natalie has identified two outcomes for this meeting. This session may take longer than the first meeting, but the group is willing to set aside as much as three hours, if necessary. She plans for one and a half hours. The intended outcomes are: A goal statement for eliminating unnecessary truck rolls and a check sheet for tracking the causes of unnecessary truck rolls. Figure A.3 shows both of these outcomes, as well as the agenda designed to achieve them.

Natalie develops the agenda to reflect what the group has to do to reach the two outcomes listed at the top. There is also a guest speaker for this meeting. Paul Evans will be present to discuss some potential causes the group might decide to track. Paul works in the corporate office and has helped some of the other CE cable systems with similar problems. The group wanted to ask him some questions, so Natalie sets aside some time on the agenda for Paul to speak to the group.

At the meeting, Natalie simply follows her agenda and applies her facilitation skills, focusing on helping group members clearly communicate their ideas about the issues. The goal statement they develop is: We will reduce unnecessary truck rolls from 21 percent to 5 percent in a way that maintains current budget levels and head count so that our workforce will be more productive and our customers will be more satisfied.

Figure A.4 shows a check sheet that is developed from this second meeting. The causes listed on the check sheet should be as detailed as possible

Figure A.3

Meeting Agenda for Cable Express
Second Meeting

Expected Outcome: A goal statement for eliminating unnecessary truck rolls and a check sheet for tracking the causes of unnecessary truck rolls.

Date: January 12

Time: 9:00 A.M.

Place: Conference room

Who Should Attend: F. Catalfamo, J. Duffy, A. Franklin, T. Hoff, L. King, M. Kensey, L. Little, B. Moss, J. Mewing, L. Palma, R. Polly, R. Ringer

What	Time	Who
Beginning of the Meeting		
1. Welcome the group	1 minutes	
2. Clarify the outcome	5 minutes	
3. Set role expectations	1 minutes	
4. Contract ground rules	30 seconds	
5. Discuss agenda	30 seconds	
Body of the Meeting		
6. Discussion with guest speaker	20 minutes	Paul Evans
7. Develop a goal statement; P phase	30 minutes	
a. Ask for ideas to complete the three phrases of a goal statement		
We will ...		
In a way that ...		
So that ...		
8. Develop a check sheet; R phase		
a. List causes of unnecessary truck rolls	15 minutes	
b. Decide who will collect the information	10 minutes	
c. Decide on the time period for collecting	5 minutes	

Figure A.3, continued
Meeting Agenda for Cable Express
Second Meeting

What	Time	Who
End of the Meeting		
9. Summarize against outcome	30 seconds	
10. Verify action items, set next meeting date	30 seconds	
11. Praise the group's effort	30 seconds	

in order to ultimately identify the exact causes that are contributing to the biggest portion of the problem. At this meeting, team members decide to meet weekly to review check sheet data from the previous week. Once they begin to notice trends, they will start to identify options for eliminating the causes that occur most often.

Natalie explains that after looking at the initial results, members may decide to gather more data before being able to determine the biggest incidences of causes. The causes listed may not be specific enough. For example, if a major factor turns out to be technician's error the first time service was performed, they might decide to gather more information by finding out which technicians were causing errors. If there were only a few technicians making mistakes, then they might need to only focus on those few technicians to correct the problem.

The group actually does meet two more times to review the check sheet results and identify any causes that need more research. This is often what occurs when involved with root cause analysis. The layers of the onion have to be peeled back, one after the other, until the root cause has been revealed. It often helps to ask the question, "Why?" For example, the CSR recorded inaccurate information about the customer's order. Why? Because the CSR did not know how to input that specific type of order. Why? Because the procedure for inputting that specific type of order is very complicated and many CSRs have trouble with it. By doing enough research to find out the REAL cause, the group will have a better chance of solving the problem.

Figure A.4

Check Sheet Developed at the Second Meeting

Unnecessary Truck Rolls

Week Ending _____

Causes	Number of Occurrences
Customer changed mind	
CSR recorded inaccurate information	
Warehouse didn't give correct parts or enough parts	
Incorrect address	
Could not find customer's house	
Truck called back due to higher priority	
Disorganized service technician	
Technician error the first time service was performed	
Customer wasn't home	
Customer wanted an additional service	
Other (please specify)	
Other	
Other	

The Fifth Meeting

In preparation for the fifth meeting Natalie considers what is currently happening and what the group will need to do next. They will be analyzing several weeks worth of data, reported in weekly increments, on causes of unnecessary truck rolls. They are ready to identify those causes that are creating the biggest problem and then decide on what actions need to take place to eliminate those causes. Natalie will use the O and B phases of PROBE to guide the group. The outcomes for this meeting will be a list of solutions to eliminate the main causes of unnecessary truck rolls and a decision on which solutions to implement. Figure A.5 illustrates the agenda that Natalie develops. The meeting will be one hour and 45 minutes long, including a break.

Figure A.5

Meeting Agenda for Cable Express
Fifth Meeting

Expected Outcome: A list of solutions for eliminating the main causes of unnecessary truck rolls and a decision on which solutions will be implemented.

Date: February 2

Time: 9:00 A.M.

Place: Conference room

Who Should Attend: F. Catalfamo, J. Duffy, A. Franklin, T. Hoff, L. King, M. Kensey, L. Little, B. Moss, J. Mewing, L. Palma, R. Polly, R. Ringer

What	Time	Who
Beginning of the Meeting		
1. Welcome the group	1 minutes	
2. Clarify the outcome and overall goal	5 minutes	
3. Set role expectations	15 seconds	
4. Contract ground rules	15 seconds	
5. Discuss agenda	30 seconds	

Figure A.5, continued

Meeting Agenda for Cable Express
Fifth Meeting

What	Time	Who
Body of the Meeting		
6. Review check sheet results	15 minutes	
7. List options; O phase		
a. Brainstorm a list of solutions	15 minutes	
b. Clarify the list of solutions	10 minutes	
c. Combine similar solutions into one	10 minutes	
Break	**10 minutes**	
8. Choose best options; B phase		
a. Eliminate the obvious	5 minutes	
b. Multi-vote to narrow the list	15 minutes	
c. Decide on options to implement	15 minutes	
End of the Meeting		
9. Summarize against outcome	1 minute	
10. Verify action items, set next meeting date	1 minute	
11. Praise the group's effort	1 minute	

During this fifth meeting, the group identifies three causes that seem to occur most often, according to the check sheet results. They are:

- The customer wasn't home
- The customer wanted an additional service and the technician had to reschedule the service call
- The technician could not find the customer's house.

There are other causes that need attention, but together, these three causes contribute to 65 percent of the unnecessary truck rolls, so the group decides to concentrate on these first.

The group decides on several solutions to eliminate the three identified causes.

First, create a mechanized phone message to send to the customer the day before the service date is scheduled. This reminds the customer of the appointment, and specifies the type of service to be done. A phone number will be included for the customer to call if there are any changes to the original order, or if the customer wants to reschedule the appointment. This will ensure that the customer is home when the technician arrives to provide service.

Next, dispatch will call the customer when the technician is on the way to the customer's home. The dispatcher can make sure the customer is there, clarify directions to the residence, and verify the service to be performed. This action will verify where the technician is going and what type of service is needed before the technician gets there.

Also, to help technicians be prepared for the unexpected, they'll be given a specified amount of additional equipment to carry on the truck and an inventory system will be developed to keep track of it. If the customer wants any service in addition to what was originally requested, it performed at the same time. Two technicians will be designated for high priority work and for delivering needed parts and equipment. In addition, they'll help if any additional service is needed that requires a lot of time.

Other solutions may be needed later, but the group decides to start with these and continue to track the truck rolls to review progress.

The Sixth Meeting

The group decides to meet within a few days of the sixth meeting, so Natalie prepares by developing an intended outcome and meeting agenda. This helps the group write an action plan for the solutions identified in the last meeting. She will be guiding the group through the last phase of PROBE, E or Execution phase. The process tool she will use is the action plan time line. The intended outcome she develops is an action plan time line for implementing the solutions to reduce unnecessary truck rolls. Figure A.6 shows the agenda she will use to facilitate the group through the process. The meeting will be two hours and ten minutes long, including a break.

Figure A.6

Meeting Agenda for Cable Express
Sixth Meeting

Expected Outcome: An action plan time line for implementing the solutions to reduce unnecessary truck rolls

Date: February 5

Time: 9:00 A.M.

Place: Conference room

Who Should Attend: F. Catalfamo, J. Duffy, A. Franklin, T. Hoff, L. King, M. Kensey, L. Little, B. Moss, J. Mewing, L. Palma, R. Polly, R. Ringer

What	Time	Who
Beginning of the Meeting		
1. Welcome the group	15 seconds	
2. Clarify the outcome and overall goal	10 minutes	
3. Set role expectations	1 minute	
4. Contract ground rules	15 seconds	
5. Discuss agenda	30 seconds	
Body of the Meeting		
6. Review the four solutions decided on in previous meeting	15 minutes	
7. Develop an action plan time line; E phase		
a. Identify the actions needed to implement the four solutions	25 minutes	
Break	**10 minutes**	
b. Clarify actions for understanding	15 minutes	
c. Eliminate actions that won't work	5 minutes	
d. Place the actions in sequential order	15 minutes	

Figure A.6, continued

Meeting Agenda for Cable Express
Sixth Meeting

What	Time	Who
e. Assign who is responsible for which action	15 minutes	
f. Assign a completion date for each action	10 minutes	
g. Reach a consensus on the actions	5 minutes	
End of the Meeting		
8. Summarize against outcome	15 seconds	
9. Verify action items, set next meeting date	30 seconds	
10. Praise the group's effort	15 seconds	

When the meeting is over, the group is able to begin implementing their plan, which is shown in Figure A.7. This is the action plan time line they will be following to reduce the unnecessary truck rolls.

Now that the action plan time line has been created and the group has made commitments as to the action items and the time frames, Natalie's job for this portion of the effort is accomplished. The group will need to continue to monitor its effort to ensure members are meeting the objective that was set in the goal statement. Natalie will continue to monitor progress and be available to assist if needed.

Summary

This section has given you a realistic example of how all the principles discussed in this book can come together to help you make improvements in your organization. Cable Express is a fictitious company, but it possesses many of the problems and challenges that real organizations face.

Figure A.7

Action Plan Time Line

Activity	Week 1	Week 2	Week 3	Week 4	Week 5	Who's Responsible
1. Get ideas for wording message to send to customers the night before service is scheduled	■					Ron Jay Frank
2. Create the message to be sent to customers	■					Ron Jay Frank
3. Schedule vendor to set up the new message in the system		■				Ron
4. Have dispatch employees begin verifying customer directions and ordered services on all calls to customers as the truck is on the way	■					Tom
5. Meet with warehouse and tech departments to decide on the specific extra equipment each technician will need to provide additional service		■			Lana	Bob Ann
6. Develop an inventory system to keep track of the extra equipment			■			Ann
7. Assign two technicians as floaters, create schedules, job responsibilities				■		Lana Larry
8. Inform CSRs and technicians of all the changes, along with other stakeholders			■			Ron Lana

As you facilitate meetings in your own organization, remember the following points.

1. Use the PROBE model over the course of several meetings. It is very rare to get through all the phases in the model in only one meeting. Research and data collection typically must be done over a period of time in between meetings.

2. The best route to the group's objective is always the simplest, most direct route. Use a minimum number of process tools to reach the intended outcome for each meeting.

3. Continue to remind the group of the overall goal statement, so they always keep the "big picture" in mind. For example, Cable Express was motivated to make changes because new competitors were stealing customers away. In a situation like this, the group can't afford to lose sight of the initial problem. If the improvements they have made do not reduce the customers waiting period for service in a significant manner, the group has more work yet to do.

There are some very important principles exemplified by this change effort at Cable Express. First, the responsibility for taking action does not only rest with you. Your group is responsible for its own success. As a facilitator, you can impact its success, but the group's level of commitment and ability will influence the amount of its overall success. That's because successful organizations result from everyone taking part and contributing, from the top down. No one person can carry the weight of an entire organization, yet it takes each individual person working in concert with everyone else to put forth his or her best effort. Every person wants to be successful, but they don't always know how. As a facilitator, you can help. You have an opportunity to influence others and make significant contributions to your organization. This case has illustrated one way to make this happen.

Bibliography

Auvine, Brian; Densmore, Betsy; Extrom, Mary; Poole, Scott; Shanklin, Michel. A *Manual for Group Facilitators*. Madison, Wisconsin: Wisconsin Clearinghouse, 1978.

Conway, William E. *The Quality Secret: The Right Way to Manage*. Nashua: Conway Quality, 1992.

Doyle, Michael and Straus, David. *How to Make Meetings Work*. New York: Jove Books, 1982.

Drew, Jeannine, *Mastering Meetings*. New York: McGraw-Hill, Inc., 1994.

Goldratt, Eliyahu M. *The Goal*. Great Barrington: North River Press, 1992.

Katzenbach, Jon R. and Smith, Douglas K. *The Wisdom of Teams*. New York: HarperBusiness, 1994.

Kennedy, Robert F. *Thirteen Days A Memoir of the Cuban Missile Crisis*. New York: Penguin Books USA, 1969.

Kinlaw, Dennis C. *Team-Managed Facilitation*. San Diego: Pfeiffer & Company, 1993.

Kiser, A. Glenn. *Masterful Facilitation*. New York: Amacom, 1998.

Leatherman, Dick. *The Training Trilogy — Facilitation Skills*. Amherst: Human Resource Development Press, Inc., 1990.

Mosvick, Roger K. and Nelson, Robert B. *We've Got to Start Meeting Like This!* Indianapolis: Park Avenue Productions, 1996.

Vaughan, Dianne. *The Challenger Launch Decision.* Chicago: The University of Chicago Press, 1996.

Index

A

action items, 13
action plan, 95–96, 97
active listening, 30–35, 40
    empathy response, 31
    nonverbal acknowledgment, 31
    rephrasing, 31
agenda 3, 6–8, 11, 16, 22, 43, 45, 52, 128,
    130, 136, 138

B

beginning a meeting, 8–11, 16, 128
    welcome, 8–9
behavior, 45, 65, 111–112
bird's eye view, 44
boarding ideas, 10
body of the meeting, 11–12, 16, 130
brainstorm, 12, 86–89, 97, 137
breaks, 51, 53
business opportunities, 79, 81, 96. 97
business problem, 78–79, 96, 97

C

categorize, 87, 97
check sheet, 81–82, 97, 132–135, 136
clarifying, 12, 25, 86, 89, 97, 137
closure, 33, 52

co-facilitator, 10
combine, 87, 90, 97, 137
commitment, 21, 28, 108
communication, good, 38–39, 40
compare against criteria, 91, 93–94, 98
compromise, 48–49
conflict, 57–63, 71–72, 111
    chaotic, 60, 62–63, 72
    communication style 58, 59–60,
        71–72
    content, 58, 59, 71–72
    getting stuck, 51
    healthy, 6, 72
    managing, 63
    process, 58–59, 71–72
    resolving, 68
    responses, 60–63
    submerged, 60–62, 72
consensus, 44, 47–53, 55, 65, 68–70,
    94–95, 111
    agreement, 46, 69, 123
content neutral, 23–24, 26, 27, 28
    content, 22
    content conflict, 59
    neutrality, 19, 20, 23, 46
    process, 22
contracting, 11, 16

conversation flow, 30, 36–37, 40
    equal involvement, 36–40
coordinator, 10
cost of a meeting, 2–3, 16
customers, 105–106, 114

D

Deming, Edwards W., 100

E

eliminate the obvious, 91, 97
empowerment. *See* levels of authority
ending a meeting, 12–15, 17, 130
    summarizing 12–13
ensure meeting is needed, 2–3, 16
    alternatives to meetings, 2
evaluation, self, 13–14, 17
execute, 74, 76, 95–96, 98

F

facilitator role, 20, 27, 101, 106, 110–113
facilitating the discussion, 29, 30
flexibility, 44, 52, 53–54, 55–56
flip chart, 37–38, 40, 51, 80–95
flow chart, 81, 82–85, 97, 132
    work process, 82–83
follow up, 13–15, 17
forming, 110, 114

G

goal statement, 76–80, 97–98, 132, 142, 143
ground rules, 11, 16, 22, 45, 46–47, 50, 54–55, 64, 68, 111–112, 128, 130
group norms, 111–112
    Inherent, 112
    overt, 112

I

interrupting, 25, 36, 119
    polite, 36–37
interventions, 63–71, 72, 120, 122, 124, 125
    changing behavior, 65, 66–68, 72, 122
    gaining management support, 65, 70–71, 72, 124

reaching consensus, 65, 68–70, 72, 123
situations, 65–66, 72

K

keeping the group aware, 44–47, 55

L

levels of authority, 106–107, 114

M

making decisions, x
Mehrabien, 31
    nonverbal, 50
minutes taker, 10

N

norming, 110, 111–112, 114

O

options, 74, 75, 76, 86–95, 97, 130, 136
    best options, 74, 75, 76, 91–95, 97–98, 130
outcome statement, 3–6, 11–12, 16, 22–23, 46, 52, 79–80, 128, 130, 132, 136, 138
    clarify, 9
    results, 4
ownership, 21, 27, 28, 108

P

parallel processing, 44
parameters, 9, 47, 78–80, 108
parking lot, 46, 117. *See* staying on track
performing, 110, 113, 114
personal attacks, 53, 64–65, 72, 111
preparation, 3–8, 16, 128, 130, 132, 136, 138
prioritizing, 91, 92–93, 130
PROBE, 73–98, 106, 130, 131, 138, 142
process model, 73
process oriented, 22–23, 25–26, 28
    process conflict, 59
process tools, 52, 58–59, 77
progress of group, 46
projection, 74, 75, 77–80, 97, 132

Q

questions, 30, 33–35, 40
    closed, 34–35, 40
    leading, 35
    open, 34–35, 40

R

recorder, 10
responsibility, 20
roles, 9, 10, 16
root cause analysis, 74, 75, 76, 80–86,
    97, 132–134, 136
    causes, 1, 5, 12, 137
round robin, 86–87, 97

S

sensitivity, 53–54, 55–56
sidebar conversations, 36
stakeholders, 108
staying on track, 46, 117. *See* parking
    lot
    on topic, 43
step out of role, 27, 28
storming, 110, 111, 114

T

suppliers, 105–106, 114
survey, 81, 85–86, 97
synergy, 101

tactfulness, 44, 54–55, 56
task, 45
team, 99–115, 113–114
    cross-functional, 104, 114
    functional, 104, 114
    multi-functional, 104–105, 114
    permanent, 98, 103–104, 114
    temporary, 98, 103–104, 114
timekeeper, 10
time spent in meetings, 9, 46
transparent, 44–45

U

unanimity, 47–48, 49

V

voting, 48, 49, 55
    multi-voting, 91–92, 98

ESTABLISH A FRAMEWORK
FOR EXCELLENCE
WITH THE OASIS PRESS ®

OASIS PRESS BOOKS & SOFTWARE
Celebrating 25 Years

THE OASIS PRESS

PSI RESEARCH

P.O. BOX 3727

CENTRAL POINT, OR

97502 · 0032

Fastbreaking changes in technology and the global marketplace continue to create unprecedented opportunities for businesses through the '90s and into the new millennium. However with these opportunities will also come many new challenges. Today, more than ever, businesses, especially small businesses, need to excel in all areas of operation to compete and succeed in an ever-changing world.

The Successful Business Library takes you through the '90s and beyond, helping you solve the day-to-day problems you face now, and prepares you for the unexpected problems you may be facing down the road. With any of our products, you will receive up-to-date and practical business solutions, which are easy to use and easy to understand. No jargon or theories, just solid, nuts-and-bolts information.

Whether you are an entrepreneur going into business for the first time or an experienced consultant trying to keep up with the latest rules and regulations, The Successful Business Library provides you with the step-by-step guidance, and action-oriented plans you need to succeed in today's world. As an added benefit, PSI Research/The Oasis Press® unconditionally guarantees your satisfaction with the purchase of any book or software application in our catalog.

More than a marketplace for our products, we actually provide something that many business Web sites tend to overlook... useful information!

It's no mystery that the World Wide Web is a great way for businesses to promote their products, however most commercial sites stop there. We have always viewed our site's goals a little differently. For starters, we have applied our 25 years of experience providing hands-on information to small businesses directly to our Web site. We offer current information to help you start your own business, guidelines to keep it up and running, useful federal and state-specific information (including addresses and phone numbers to contact these resources), and a forum for business owners to communicate and network with others on the Internet. We would like to invite you to check out our Web site and discover the information that can assist you and your small business venture.

The Oasis Press Online
http://www.psi-research.com

From The Leading Publisher of Small Business Information
Books that save you time and money.

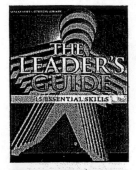

This authoritative guide will transform the roles of administrators and improve effectiveness for corporate, nonprofit, and community organizations, many of which are over-managed but lack effective leadership. Its skills-oriented solutions teach managers to be effective leaders and train leaders to be better managers — a distinction often overlooked by other management guides.

The Leader's Guide: 15 Essential Skills   **Pages: 250**
Paperback: $19.95   ISBN: 1-55571-434-X

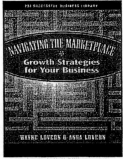

Two very practical small business books in one. Book one offers competitive strategies and offers a number of defensive business models that can be adopted, copied, or modified to fit a particular business challenge. Book two, contains fourteen strategies that guarantee sales and profits. Each model contains a competitive strategy that will lessen the impact of a competitor's action by helping target and highly satisfy one specific type of customer.

Navigating the Marketplace   **Pages: 350**
Paperback: $21.95   ISBN: 1-55571-458-7

"Advertising," says author Kathy Kobliski, "is not a perfect science. It's not even close." For many small business owners, that means the potential for wasting thousands of dollars on the wrong advertising decisions. This guide is an ideal primer on the in's and out's of advertising and how to get the information you need to pinpoint your advertising objectives. Complete with worksheets, plus help in grasping the lingo, and techniques to target your defined market with the best medium.

Advertising Without An Agency   **Pages: 175**
Paperback: $19.95   ISBN: 1-55571-429-3

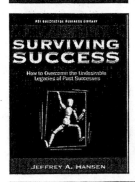

Surviving Success presents a program for those who wish to lead their companies from promising startup to industry dominance. Meet the challenges of business growth and transition with new insights. Learn from success stories. Be prepared to take proactive steps into your company's next growth transition.

Surviving Success   **Pages: 230**
Paperback: $19.95   ISBN: 1-55571-446-3

Order Directly From **The Oasis Press**®

Call, Mail, Email, or Fax Your Order to: PSI Research, P.O. Box 3727, Central Point, OR 97502
Order Phone USA & Canada: +1 800 228-2275   Email: info@psi-research.com   Fax: +1 541 476-1479

Includes Titles Through Winter 1999

TITLE	✔ BINDER	✔ PAPERBACK	QUANTITY	COST
Advertising Without An Agency: A Comprehensive Guide to Radio, Television, Print...		❏ $19.95		
Bottom Line Basics: Understand and Control Your Finances	❏ $39.95	❏ $19.95		
BusinessBasics: A Microbusiness Startup Guide		❏ $16.95		
The Business Environmental Handbook	❏ $39.95	❏ $19.95		
Business Owner's Guide to Accounting & Bookkeeping		❏ $19.95		
businessplan.com: how to write a web-woven strategic business plan		❏ $19.95		
Buyer's Guide to Business Insurance	❏ $39.95	❏ $19.95		
California Corporation Formation Package		❏ $29.95		
Collection Techniques for a Small Business	❏ $39.95	❏ $19.95		
A Company Policy and Personnel Workbook	❏ $49.95	❏ $29.95		
Company Relocation Handbook	❏ $39.95	❏ $19.95		
CompControl: The Secrets of Reducing Workers' Compensation Costs	❏ $39.95	❏ $19.95		
Complete Book of Business Forms		❏ $19.95		
Connecting Online: Creating a Successful Image on the Internet		❏ $21.95		
Customer Engineering: Cutting Edge Selling Strategies	❏ $39.95	❏ $19.95		
Develop & Market Your Creative Ideas		❏ $15.95		
Developing International Markets: Shaping Your Global Presence		❏ $19.95		
Doing Business in Russia: Basic Facts for the Pioneering Entrepreneur		❏ $19.95		
Draw The Line: A Sexual Harassment Free Workplace		❏ $17.95		
Entrepreneurial Decisionmaking: A Survival Manual for the Next Millennium		❏ $21.95		
The Essential Corporation Handbook		❏ $21.95		
The Essential Limited Liability Company Handbook	❏ $39.95	❏ $21.95		
Export Now: A Guide for Small Business	❏ $39.95	❏ $24.95		
Financial Decisionmaking: A CPA/Attorney's Perspective		❏ $19.95		
Financial Management Techniques for Small Business	❏ $39.95	❏ $19.95		
Financing Your Small Business: Techniques for Planning, Acquiring, & Managing Debt		❏ $19.95		
Franchise Bible: How to Buy a Franchise or Franchise Your Own Business	❏ $39.95	❏ $24.95		
Friendship Marketing: Growing Your Business by Cultivating Strategic Relationships		❏ $18.95		
Funding High-Tech Ventures		❏ $21.95		
Home Business Made Easy		❏ $19.95		
Information Breakthrough: How to Turn Mountains of Confusing Data into Gems of Useful Information		❏ $22.95		
Improving Staff Productivity: Ideas to increase Profits		❏ $16.95		
The Insider's Guide to Small Business Loans		❏ $19.95		
InstaCorp – Incorporate In Any State (Book & Software)		❏ $29.95		
Joysticks, Blinking Lights and Thrills		❏ $18.95		
Keeping Score: An Inside Look at Sports Marketing		❏ $18.95		
Know Your Market: How to Do Low-Cost Market Research	❏ $39.95	❏ $19.95		
The Leader's Guide: 15 Essential Skills		❏ $19.95		
Legal Expense Defense: How to Control Your Business' Legal Costs and Problems	❏ $39.95	❏ $19.95		
Legal Road Map for Consultants		❏ $18.95		
Location, Location, Location: How to Select the Best Site for Your Business		❏ $19.95		
Mail Order Legal Guide	❏ $45.00	❏ $29.95		
Managing People: A Practical Guide		❏ $21.95		
Marketing for the New Millennium: Applying New Techniques		❏ $19.95		
Marketing Mastery: Your Seven Step Guide to Success	❏ $39.95	❏ $19.95		
The Money Connection: Where and How to Apply for Business Loans and Venture Capital	❏ $39.95	❏ $24.95		
Moonlighting: Earn a Second Income at Home		❏ $15.95		
Navigating the Marketplace: Growth Strategies For Your Business		❏ $21.95		
No Money Down Financing for Franchising		❏ $19.95		
People Investment: How to Make Your Hiring Decisions Pay Off For Everyone	❏ $39.95	❏ $19.95		
Power Marketing for Small Business	❏ $39.95	❏ $19.95		
Profit Power: 101 Pointers to Give Your Business a Competitive Edge		❏ $19.95		
Proposal Development: How to Respond and Win the Bid	❏ $39.95	❏ $21.95		
Public Relations Marketing: Making a Splash Without Much Cash		❏ $19.95		
Raising Capital: How to Write a Financing Proposal		❏ $19.95		
Renaissance 2000: Liberal Arts Essentials for Tomorrow's Leaders		❏ $22.95		
Retail in Detail: How to Start and Manage a Small Retail Business		❏ $15.95		
Secrets of High Ticket Selling		❏ $19.95		
Secrets to Buying and Selling a Business		❏ $24.95		
Secure Your Future: Financial Planning at Any Age	❏ $39.95	❏ $19.95		
Selling Services: A Guide for the Consulting Professional		❏ $18.95		
The Small Business Insider's Guide to Bankers		❏ $18.95		
BOOK SUB-TOTAL (Additional titles on other side)				

TITLE	✔ BINDER	✔ PAPERBACK	QUANTITY	COST
SmartStart Your (State) Business... series		❑ $19.95		
Please specify which state(s) you would like:				
Smile Training Isn't Enough: The Three Secrets to Excellent Customer Service		❑ $19.95		
Start Your Business (Also available as a book and disk package, see below)		❑ $ 9.95 *(without disk)*		
Successful Network Marketing for The 21st Century		❑ $15.95		
Surviving Success: Managing the Challenges of Growth		❑ $19.95		
TargetSmart! Database Marketing for the Small Business		❑ $19.95		
Top Tax Saving Ideas for Today's Small Business		❑ $16.95		
Twenty-One Sales in a Sale: What Sales Are You Missing?		❑ $19.95		
Which Business? Help in Selecting Your New Venture		❑ $18.95		
Write Your Own Business Contracts		❑ $24.95		
BOOK SUB-TOTAL (Don't forget to include your amount from the previous side)				

OASIS SOFTWARE Please specify which computer operating system you use (DOS, Mac OS, or Windows)

TITLE	✔ Windows	✔ Mac OS	QUANTITY	COST
California Corporation Formation Package ASCII Software	❑ $ 39.95	❑ $ 39.95		
Company Policy & Personnel Software Text Files	❑ $ 49.95	❑ $ 49.95		
Financial Management Techniques (Full Standalone)	❑ $ 99.95			
Financial Templates	❑ $ 69.95	❑ $ 69.95		
The Insurance Assistant Software (Full Standalone)	❑ $ 29.95			
Start Your Business (Software for Windows™)	❑ $ 19.95			
The Survey Genie - Customer Edition (Full Standalone)	❑ $199.95 (WIN)	❑ $149.95 (DOS)		
The Survey Genie - Employee Edition (Full Standalone)	❑ $199.95 (WIN)	❑ $149.95 (DOS)		
Winning Business Plans in Color (MS Office Addition)	❑ $ 39.95			
SOFTWARE SUB-TOTAL				

BOOK & DISK PACKAGES Please specify which computer operating system you use (DOS, Mac OS, or Windows)

TITLE	✔ Windows	✔ MacOS	✔ Binder	✔ Paperback	QUANTITY	COST
The Buyer's Guide to Business Insurance w/ Insurance Assistant	❑		❑ $ 59.95	❑ $ 39.95		
California Corporation Formation Book & Text Files	❑	❑		❑ $ 59.95		
Company Policy & Personnel Book & Software Text Files	❑	❑	❑ $ 89.95	❑ $ 69.95		
Financial Management Techniques Book & Software	❑		❑ $129.95	❑ $ 119.95		
Start Your Business Paperback & Software (Software for Windows™)	❑			❑ $ 24.95		
BOOK & DISK PACKAGE SUB-TOTAL						

SOLD TO: Please give street address for shipping.

Name:

Title:

Company:

Street Address:

City/State/Zip:

Daytime Phone: Email:

SHIP TO: If different than above, please give alternate street address

Name:

Company:

Street Address:

City/State/Zip:

Daytime Phone:

GRAND TOTAL

SUB-TOTALS *(from other side)*	$	
SUB-TOTALS *(from this side)*	$	
SHIPPING (see chart below)	$	
TOTAL ORDER	**$**	

If your purchase is:	Shipping costs within the USA:
$0 - $25	$5.00
$25.01 - $50	$6.00
$50.01 - $100	$7.00
$100.01 - $175	$9.00
$175.01 - $250	$13.00
$250.01 - $500	$18.00
$500.01 +	4% of total merchandise

**You can also order online
24-hours a day and 7 days a week at
http://www.psi-research.com**

PAYMENT INFORMATION: *Rush service is available, call for details.*
International and Canadian Orders: *Please call 1-541-479-9464 for quote on shipping.*
Please indicate a method of payment below:

❑ **CHECK** *Enclosed, payable to PSI Research*   ❑ **VISA**   ❑ **MASTERCARD**   ❑ **AMEX**   ❑ **DISCOVER**

Card Number: Expires:

Signature: Name On Card: